THE

ALLOCATION PROBLEM

in

Financial Accounting Theory

by

ARTHUR L. THOMAS, PH.D., CPA
Professor of Accounting, McMaster University

AMERICAN ACCOUNTING ASSOCIATION

THE ALLOCATION PROBLEM
in
FINANCIAL ACCOUNTING THEORY

AMERICAN ACCOUNTING ASSOCIATION

THE By-Laws of the American Accounting Association state that the first purpose of the Association shall be "To initiate, encourage, and sponsor research in accounting and to publish or aid in the publication of the results of research." In harmony with this objective, the publication of the Studies in Accounting Research is aimed at encouraging and publishing research. This series is an outgrowth of the research program initiated by the Association in 1965. Under this program, research projects and authors are selected by the Director of Research, who is assisted by a three-man Research Advisory Committee.

When the project is commissioned, the author is allowed maximum freedom in conducting research. The author is solely responsible for the procedures followed and the research conclusions. An Editorial Consulting Committee is appointed for each project. Members of this Committee are expected to suggest ideas and offer comments on the scope of the project, the methodology, and the researcher's findings. They are not empowered to block publication, nor may they insert dissents in the final report; they are advisory only. The Editorial Consulting Committee for the project is:

WILLIAM H. BEAVER	University of Chicago
G. O. BIERWAG	University of Oregon
R. GENE BROWN	Syntex Laboratories, Inc.
EDWIN H. CAPLAN	University of New Mexico
JOEL S. DEMSKI	Stanford University
MELVIN GREENBALL	The Ohio State University
ELDON S. HENDRIKSEN	Washington State University
H. T. KOPLIN	University of Oregon
JOHN LESLIE LIVINGSTONE	The Ohio State University
CHRIS J. LUNESKI	University of Oregon
RENE MANES	Purdue University
ROBERT R. STERLING	University of Kansas

This project was commissioned by Robert K. Jaedicke (Stanford University) when he was Director of Research. The Research Advisory Committee at that time was Harold Bierman, Jr., (Cornell University), Carl L. Nelson (Columbia University), and Charles T. Zlatkovich (University of Texas).

October 1969

Acknowledgments

I WISH to express my deep appreciation of the efforts of my editor, Robert K. Jaedicke, and the Project Editorial Consulting Committee. The magnitude of their contribution is reflected in the complete rewriting (and doubling in length) that this study has undergone since their initial responses to it were received. Individual committee members will recognize passages where their comments have been directly incorporated in the revised text.

I owe special debts to Eldon S. Hendriksen and David A. Baerncopf, both of whom have provided detailed criticism of this book from its inception, and much-needed encouragement. Encouragement from Harold Bierman, Jr., at a particular point also was vital in this book's reaching its present form.

I am grateful to my former colleagues Paul Frishkoff, Dale S. Harwood, Charles E. Johnson, Arthur E. Mace, Franklin L. McCarthy, William H. Parks, James E. Reinmuth, Larry E. Richards, Donald S. Tull, Rajwant Singh, Ronald Curry, and Earl K. Littrell (the last of whom served both as research assistant and as a source of ideas and examples). Some of the preliminary research behind this study was supported by a Faculty Summer Research Award from the Office of Scientific and Scholarly Research of the University of Oregon.

This book grew out of criticism of an earlier work of mine by Stephen A. Zeff, and conversations during 1962 and 1963 with William J. Schlatter and W. Allen Spivey at the University of Michigan. In one form or another its materials have been presented in talks or workshops at Harpur College, Ohio State University, Simon Fraser University, the University of Alberta, the University of British Columbia, the University of Buffalo, the University of Kansas, and a regional workshop of accounting researchers. Comments and suggestions received at these gatherings have been very helpful in the evolution of this study, as have written comments received from R. J. Chambers, Reg S. Gynther, Daniel L. McDonald, Carl L. Nelson, Lawrence A. Sherr, and George J. Staubus. Also, I am deeply indebted to the various authors whose works are cited in the text, as well as to those many others not cited whose writing provided the background to my thinking. Readers familiar with the literature will recognize that my perception of what accountants do has been deeply influenced by the writings of William J. Vatter.

The present form of the book owes much to the editing of Dr. Anne C. Garrison of Michigan State University, who also provided numerous useful suggestions for tightening its arguments.

Finally, I wish to thank my wife, Mary, for her hours of proofreading, for her patience during periods when this project was going badly, and generally for her help and support.

Hamilton, Ontario
September, 1969

To

William J. Schlatter

Life is not so simple as crossing a field.—Traditional Slavic proverb

Table of Contents

problems result from uncertainty and lack of data. But, as will be demonstrated, this problem would plague financial accounting even under conditions of certainty and omniscience.

The conclusions reached are unavoidably tentative. Under *present* allocation theory it usually will be impossible to defend the kinds of allocations that financial accountants *currently* wish to make. But at any time an improvement in allocation theory may occur, or the profession may adopt a new approach to financial accounting that avoids the necessity for arbitrary allocations.

A note on the bibliographical cutoff

Fairly heavy reference is made in what follows to the theoretical literature of accounting. The topic of allocation is being actively discussed at present; each new issue of the major journals brings additional material. A cutoff was required. Accordingly, no materials received after July 1, 1968, have been referred to in this study.

Introduction

THIS study concerns the financial accounting treatment of nonmonetary inputs: depreciable assets, inventories, prepayments, labor services, research and development, advertising, and the like. It concerns the timing of writeoff of such inputs to expense or to cost of goods manufactured. It concerns the calculation of the amounts used to represent some of these inputs as assets on the balance sheet. Financial accounting theorists have been arguing matters relating to the treatment of such inputs for more than three-quarters of a century. These disputes are major factors in the general problems of cost accumulation and of matching costs with revenues.[1]

Why have these problems been so difficult to settle? Reasons usually offered include the uncertainty of the related estimates, the need to allow for varying circumstances of different companies, and so forth. These are indeed serious problems. But there is another that is even more fundamental. *The inputs interact, and their interaction prevents theoretical justification from being given to the input allocations employed in financial accounting.* The importance of input interactions to accounting has not yet been widely recognized. Much of this book is spent demonstrating how and why these interactions are significant. The arguments are complicated, and the following summary of them is unavoidably rough.

1. It is demonstrated that accountants at present either amortize the costs of nonmonetary assets in an arbitrary manner, or else allocate these costs in a pattern which conforms to the pattern of the input's effects on income (or to a corresponding pattern of cash-flow effects).

2. If an allocation is employed, the accountant first allocates income to one or more individual inputs, then uses the resulting pattern of income effects to determine a *second* allocation pattern, whereby the cost of the nonmonetary input is allocated to one or more years.

3. Present allocation theory provides only a few ways to conduct allocations. It is demonstrated that all of these approaches lead to arbitrary results if inputs interact. The accountant's allocation problem here is similar to that of one who would allocate the services of a watch to its individual parts. It is always mechanically possible to conduct *some* kind of allocation, but the results are apt to be meaningless.

4. Input interaction is widespread. Accordingly, at present reported magnitudes for nonmonetary inputs and related expenses will usually be arbitrary, and can be no better justified than any of a wide variety of other possible magnitudes. The significance of related asset and expense data will be impossible to specify.

---

[1] This book employs various conventional terms commonly used by accountants. Certain of these either are inexact or are loosely applied in the accounting literature. This book demonstrates that *matching* is such a term. Others include such words and phrases as *materiality, going concern,* and *cash flow.*

Inexact or ambiguous language confuses issues; I have tried to avoid using such terms. But from time to time they are needed—for instance, to indicate the implications of arguments or conclusions for certain matters of traditional concern to accountants. Several readers of earlier versions of this study suggested that when such terms *are* used, they be set off in quotes. But doing so makes for choppy exposition. Instead, it seems preferable to say at the outset that I am aware of the limitations of such language, and have tried to confine its use to places where precision is unimportant.

Outline of chapters

Chapter One examines the ways in which accountants amortize nonmonetary assets and demonstrates that the processes *are* ones of allocation; Chapter One also discusses the minimum requirements for giving theoretical justification to an allocation method. Chapter Two surveys the various approaches to allocation presently being used or proposed by accountants; for simplicity, depreciable assets are chosen as a specific example of the general problem. It is demonstrated that conventional depreciation must employ an approach designated the "net-revenue-contributions" approach, or else be arbitrary.

Chapters Three and Four examine two different forms of this approach, and the difficulties created for them by input interactions within individual years. Chapter Five extends this discussion to interaction effects between years, and concludes that, except under unusual circumstances, the net-revenue-contributions approach must be arbitrary in the presence of input interactions. Therefore (since it has been previously demonstrated that all other conventional approaches must be arbitrary, too) it is concluded that in the presence of input interactions *all* conventional approaches to input allocation must be arbitrary.

Chapter Six examines the various unconventional approaches to financial accounting that have been proposed by theorists. Here it is argued that, in the present states of accounting theory and allocation theory, if financial accounting is to avoid being arbitrary it must do one of two things:

1. Financial accounting might avoid making allocations. It is shown that two unconventional methods satisfy this requirement, but that both in effect lead to abandoning the effort to measure income (at least as that effort is usually perceived). These two methods are the current-price approaches recommended by Chambers and Sterling, and the substitution of net-quick-asset funds statements for income statements.

2. Financial accounting might attempt to base allocations on rules upon which intelligent laymen would agree. Unfortunately, it is shown that neither accountants nor users of financial statements would be satisfied with the results that probably would flow from this approach.

Finally, this book concludes with a brief discussion of possible weaknesses in its own arguments.

It will be demonstrated that present theory makes all attempts to justify the treatment given to nonmonetary inputs ultimately rest upon efforts to allocate portions of the costs of these inputs to benefits received from them by the firm. The particular concept of "benefit" involved here ultimately relates to an increase in the entity's income (or decrease in losses), or to closely related cash-flow notions.

Under what circumstances will such cost-to-benefit allocations be theoretically justified? This study argues that under *present* allocation theory, the firm's revenue function (relating its inputs to its revenues) must be free of significant interaction effects; otherwise such allocations are arbitrary. Yet, at the level of disaggregation found in financial accounting, interaction effects are widespread and important.

It should be emphasized that this problem is one of basic theory, having to do with violations of essential underlying assumptions of allocation. It is not a problem that can be solved by empirical research, though empirical research could help determine the exact present dimensions of this problem. Other widely recognized allocation

CHAPTER ONE

The Nature of the Problem

I. The Roots of the Problem

THE allocation problem in financial accounting has many of its roots in the concepts that underlie our notions of assets, expenses, and the like—and in the ways in which we associate numbers with these notions. The first part of this chapter is an elementary description of what the profession presently is doing in its reports. I will not be concerned until later with the alternative practices being proposed by accounting theorists. But (as will be demonstrated in Chapter Six) the conclusions reached in this chapter apply equally well to most of these proposed alternatives.

A word of caution is important. Various authorities are cited for the observations made in this chapter.[1] But the matters at issue are not ones that can be settled simply by reference to authority. Instead, it is important that the reader *satisfy himself* from his own experience of financial accounting and its literature that a fair (though somewhat simplified) description of present practices has been given.

Economic goods

The accountant's notion of an asset is closely related to the economist's concept of an economic good. A *good* is *anything* wanted or desired by some entity, or capable of satisfying some entity's wants, whether it be a physical thing (like a building), a service, or whatever. The economist narrows this notion by restricting his attention to *economic goods*, which are goods that can be bought and sold in a market—goods that command a price. To command a price they must be scarce—any good that is readily available, free, is not an economic good.[2]

Some economic goods are either cash itself or a legally enforceable claim to receive cash. These may be called *monetary* goods. All other economic goods may be called *nonmonetary*. Nonmonetary economic goods include buildings, advertising campaigns, services of skilled mechanics, merchandise inventories, fire insurance policies, results

[1] Primary reliance is placed on the following standard references, though other sources are cited in the body of the discussion: Rufus Wixon and Walter G. Kell, editors, *Accountants' Handbook* (New York: the Ronald Press Company, 1960), Chapters 1, 11, 12, 16, 17; Robert T. Sprouse and Maurice Moonitz, *A Tentative Set of Broad Accounting Principles for Business Enterprises*, Accounting Research Study No. 3 (New York: American Institute of Certified Public Accountants, 1962), Chapters 1, 3, 4, 6; Eric L. Kohler, *A Dictionary for Accountants*, Third Edition (Englewood Cliffs, New Jersey: Prentice-Hall, Inc., 1963), various entries; Paul Grady, *Inventory of Generally Accepted Accounting Principles for Business Enterprises*, Accounting Research Study No. 7 (New York: American Institute of Certified Public Accountants, 1965), Chapters 2, 4, 6, 11; Eldon S. Hendriksen, *Accounting Theory* (Homewood, Illinois: Richard D. Irwin, Inc., 1965), Chapters 6 and 8; and the following reports of committees of the American Accounting Association: "Accounting and Reporting Standards for Corporate Financial Statements—1957 Revision," *Accounting Review*, XXXII (October, 1957), 536–46; "Accounting for Land, Buildings, and Equipment," *Accounting Review*, XXXIX (July, 1964), 693–99; "A Discussion of Various Approaches to Inventory Measurement," *Accounting Review*, XXXIX (July, 1964), 700–14; "The Realization Concept," *Accounting Review*, XL (April, 1965), 312–22; and "The Matching Concept," *Accounting Review*, XL (April, 1965), 368–72.

[2] Technically, for a good *not* to be an economic good it must be readily available, free, *in the location where it is desired, and without effort*. As an example, wild rice is readily available, free, but it commands a high price because of the difficulties of gathering it.

of research and development efforts . . . *any* economic goods that are neither cash nor legally enforceable claims to receive cash.[3] Although there are allocation problems associated with monetary goods,[4] we will see that some especially difficult allocation problems in financial accounting relate to nonmonetary goods. The remainder of this study concentrates on these problems of *non*monetary goods allocation.

The accountant's notion of a nonmonetary *asset* takes the theoretical concept of a nonmonetary economic good and narrows it down, attempting to give it operational content in the process. First, financial statements report economic data about individual economic entities. An accounting asset is not just an economic good, but a good that is of economic significance *to the particular entity* preparing the financial statements upon which the asset is reflected.[5] The significance of the asset consists of its promise of offering future economic benefits or services to the entity.[6] The entity must have a legally enforceable claim to receive these benefits or services.[7] If a good does *not* offer such services to the entity, it is not an asset of that entity. (The reverse is not always true: for example advertising services contracted for in one year, but to be received and paid for in the next year, ordinarily would not be reported as an asset.)

Present accounting practice imposes some additional restrictions. Accountants wish to represent economic phenomena by numbers.[8] With minor exceptions (such as gift assets), accountants wish initially to record nonmonetary goods at their acquisition prices to the entity.[9] Under present accounting rules, the allocation problem arises when a nonmonetary economic good's estimated services to the entity are of limited duration, but of a duration greater than a single accounting period; the problem is to determine how much of the acquisition price should be associated with each period.

Three kinds of economic goods

For simplicity, the following discussion will assume calendar-year accounting periods. (If need be, the conclusions reached can easily enough be modified to handle cases of quarterly and other non-annual reporting.) The *service life* of a nonmonetary economic good is the number of years during which it is assumed that the good will

---

[3] For a non-cash asset to be a monetary asset, it must satisfy both the requirement of being a claim to receive cash *and* of being a legally enforceable claim. For example, the holder of a fire insurance policy has at most a *contingent* claim to receive cash, until a fire occurs; therefore, a fire insurance policy is classified as nonmonetary. (If a fire does occur, there then will be a receivable from the insurance company—a monetary asset—but this is a different asset from the policy itself.)

[4] These include amortization of bond discount and premium, the timing of profit recognition on installment sales, and the like. There are also less widely acknowledged problems of allocating costs of holding monetary items, extending credit, and so forth.

[5] It also, of course, is a good *owned* by the entity (with occasional exceptions for such things as mortgaged assets).

[6] "Assets are economic resources devoted to business purposes within a specific accounting entity; they are aggregates of service-potentials available for or beneficial to expected operations."—AAA (1957), p. 538; see also AAA (Land), p. 694; AAA (Matching), p. 368; Sprouse and Moonitz (1962), pp. 19–23, 32–33; Grady (1965), pp. 99–102, 148–49; and Hendriksen (1965), pp. 194–95.

[7] Hendriksen (1965), pp. 194–95. Note that, cash excepted, both monetary and nonmonetary assets involve legally enforceable claims—in the one case to receive cash, in the other to receive services.

[8] See Hendriksen (1965), p. 195.

[9] Wixon and Kell (1960), pp. (1–16), (1–17), (16–2)-(16–5); Kohler (1963), pp. 14–17; Grady (1965), pp. 27, 229; Hendriksen (1965), pp. 196–97. As we will see later in this chapter, this "acquisition price" is the sum of: a) any cash paid or liability assumed to acquire the good; and, b) all, or parts of, the acquisition prices of any *other* goods given up or allocated to the particular economic good under consideration.

provide economic services to the entity.[10] In effect, accountants divide all nonmonetary economic goods into three classes.

1. *Unlimited-life goods.* Some nonmonetary economic goods, most notably industrial site land, are regarded as having unlimited service lives. Under present accounting rules, if an entity has purchased such a good, and services are expected from it for an unlimited period, the accountant will report this good as an asset, and will (in current and subsequent years) associate with it a number that equals its original acquisition price.

2. *Single-year goods.* At the other extreme, the services of some nonmonetary economic goods are considered to be expended between the date of their acquisition and the date at which financial statements are prepared. Newspaper advertising paid for on December 12th and run on December 17th would be an example of a single-year good.[11] Similar advertising paid for on December 12th to be run next January 4th would be an example of a good that was *not* regarded as single-year. Under present accounting rules, a single-year good is handled in one of two possible ways:

a) If the expenditure of its services is perceived as relating to the acquisition of some other nonmonetary economic good (which will provide services to the entity), then the acquisition price of the single-year good will be included in the acquisition price of the other economic good. An example of this is the inclusion of the costs of raw materials in the costs of a manufactured inventory.[12]

b) If no other nonmonetary economic good is perceived to result from expenditure of the single-year good's services, then the acquisition price of the single-year good is treated as an expense or a loss on the current year's income statement.

In neither event is the single-year good *per se* reported as an asset on the entity's financial statements—though similar goods may be reported *per se* as assets if, like the January 4th advertising, their services to the entity happen to be expended in a year other than the year of acquisition.[13]

3. *Multi-year goods.* In contrast, a multi-year good is any nonmonetary economic good of limited service life which the accountant treats as yielding services to the entity during at least one year subsequent to its year of acquisition. (A multi-year good may also be defined negatively as any recognized good which is *not* treated as single-year or unlimited-life.) In the previous example, the January 4th advertising was a multi-year good. So is a building.

Under present "generally accepted" accounting rules, the acquisition price of a

---

[10] The next chapter will develop a more precise definition of the nature of economic services in accounting. However, it might be mentioned here that if a good has a scrap value at the end of its service life, receipt of that scrap value is of course one final economic service that it provides to the entity.

[11] Notice that single-year goods are defined here in terms of the *treatment* they receive under present accounting rules, not in terms of their actual economic services. The *benefits* of advertising may extend beyond the year in which the advertisement is run, but the accountant usually chooses to ignore this and to *treat* the advertising as a single-year good. The terminology used in this chapter is descriptive, not normative; it is concerned with what accountants *are* doing, not with what they possibly should be doing.

[12] Wixon and Kell (1960), p. (1–17); Sprouse and Moonitz (1962), p. 49.

[13] Wixon and Kell (1960) pp. (12–3), (12–23). Notice, finally, that the definition of single-year goods relates to the way in which goods are reported (or not reported) on the entity's *financial statements*. The single-year good never appears on the financial statements as an asset. But nothing is said here about the ways in which these goods may be recorded on the entity's *books*. For example, merchandise inventories acquired and sold within the same year often are initially *recorded* as assets, then expensed when sold. But from the vantage point of the published financial statements, such inventories are not reported as assets, so they are single-year goods.

multi-year good is handled in much the same way *over its entire service life* as is the acquisition price of a single-year good during its single year: it either is incorporated in the acquisition prices of one or more other economic goods, or is expensed (or treated as a loss). *During* the service life of a multi-year good, the accountant assigns portions of its acquisition price to the income statements or to other economic goods acquired at least one year subsequent to the year of the good's acquisition.

At the end of the year of the good's acquisition (and perhaps at the ends of one or more subsequent years) this allocation will be incomplete; the good is then reported as an *asset*, at an amount equal to the unallocated portion of its acquisition price.

Expired costs (expenses) to be charged against the curent period's revenue . . . must be distinguished from unexpired costs (inventories, prepaid and deferred costs, and fixed assets) to be charged against the revenue of future periods in order to present net income fairly.[14]

Why are the acquisition prices of these goods allocated to years other than the year of acquisition? In part because, were they not, the entity's net income could fluctuate widely from year to year, even though other economic activity remained constant both in intensity and profitability; in part, for reasons discussed in the next chapter: costs are allocated to those revenues which the goods are perceived as having *caused*, or to the periods that the goods are deemed to have benefitted.[15] Such goods include the following (the sense in which inventories are included is discussed below):

Buildings	Inventories of merchandise, finished
Equipment	goods, and supplies
Leases and patents	Prepaid insurance, and many other
Mineral deposits	kinds of prepayments

An even more interesting question is: why are many similar-seeming goods usually allocated only to the year of acquisition? These goods include:

Our previous example of advertising campaigns (since the indirect benefits probably extend beyond one year)
Research and development expenditures
Improved efficiency expected from providing special training to employees

Reasons usually given are that the future benefits are uncertain and that the necessary estimates are too subjective, or arbitrary, for allocation to be meaningful.[16] The treatment given such a good may depend on the accountant as well as upon the the the nature of the good itself. This is particularly evident with certain expenditures for research and development, where present "generally accepted" rules allow either capitalizing the expenditure or expensing it in the current year.

Summary of nonmonetary economic good allocations[17]

Here, then, is a summary of how the financial accountant allocates the acquisition prices of nonmonetary economic goods:

---

[14] Grady (1965), p. 100; see also pp. 102, 228; and Wixon and Kell (1960), pp. (1–18), (11–59), (16–2), (16–7).

[15] Wixon and Kell (1960), p. (16–6).

[16] Wixon and Kell (1960), pp. (12-3), (12-4), (12-7); Grady (1965), p. 101; Hendriksen (1965), pp. 152–53.

[17] Grady provides a convenient, if simplified, summary of the accountant's treatment of limited-life nonmonetary economic goods:

"Expenses are costs which have expired in the process of producing revenue or with the passage of time. The term 'cost' here means the sum of applicable expenditures and charges, directly or indirectly incurred, in ac-

1. *Unlimited-life goods.* So long as these are owned by the entity, the acquisition prices are not allocated. If eventually sold, the acquisition prices are allocated to the year of sale.

2. *Single-year goods.* The entire acquisition price is allocated to the year of acquisition (either to the expenses or losses of that year, or to the acquisition prices of other economic goods acquired during that year).

3. *Multi-year goods.* The acquisition price is allocated to at least one year other than the year of acquisition, and often to many such years. Part of the acquisition price may be allocated to the year of acquisition. (Once again, allocations may be either to expenses or losses, or to the acquisition prices of other economic goods.)

Finally, the acquisition price of a nonmonetary asset will be the sum of any cash paid or liability assumed to acquire the good, plus any allocations of the acquisition prices of other nonmonetary economic goods that were made in the manner indicated above.

Inventories

A bit more needs to be said about inventories. Usually supplies, merchandise, raw materials, and finished goods are acquired in batches, or *lots*, rather than by the individual item.[18] In this sense, the acquisition price of, say, a particular raw material may be allocated to more than one year, or to several other economic goods. An advantage to perceiving things this way is that it becomes evident that the accountant's problems with differing inventory and depreciation methods are really forms of the same allocation problem—though, as it were, at different points along a continuum. (In both cases the problem is to determine what portion of an acquisition price should

---

quiring a good or service in the condition and location in which it is used or sold. Initially, cost incurrence produces an asset or provides a service, the benefits of which are expected to produce present or future revenues. As the benefits are used up or expire, the portion of the cost applicable to the revenues realized is charged against revenue."
—Grady (1965), pp. 99–100. For further background, see Wixon and Kell (1960), pp. (1–15)–(1–18), (11–59)–(11–61), (12-2)–(12-4); Sprouse and Moonitz (1962), pp. 8–9; Kohler (1963), pp. 144–46, 162–63, 208; Grady (1965), pp. 74, 99–102, 228, 409, 433–44; Hendriksen (1965), pp. 142, 151–54, 192–97; AAA (1957), pp. 539–41; AAA (Matching), pp. 368–70; William A. Paton and A. C. Littleton, *An Introduction to Corporate Accounting Standards* (Columbus, Ohio: American Accounting Association, 1940), pp. 10–18, 24–27, 33, 65–74, 77, 81–85, 88–93; William J. Vatter, *The Fund Theory of Accounting and Its Implications for Financial Reports* (Chicago: University of Chicago Press, 1947), pp. 14–19; Oscar S. Gellein, "The Decreasing-Charge Concept," *Journal of Accountancy*, C (August, 1955), pp. 56–57; Carl Thomas Devine, *Essays in Accounting Theory* (privately printed, 1962), II, 258–70, 338–41; Earl A. Spiller, Jr., "Theory and Practice in the Development of Accounting," *Accounting Review*, XXXIX (October, 1964), 850–59; Glenn L. Johnson, "The Monetary and Nonmonetary Distinction," *Accounting Review*, XL (October, 1965), 821–23; Delmer P. Hylton, "On Matching Revenue With Expense," *Accounting Review*, XL (October 1965), 824–28; Willard J. Graham, "Some Observations on the Nature of Income, Generally Accepted Accounting Principles, and Financial Reporting," *Law and Contemporary Problems*, XXX (Autumn, 1965), 660–64; Morton Backer, "The Measurement of Business Income, Part I—The Matching Concept," in Morton Backer, editor, *Modern Accounting Theory* (Englewood Cliffs, New Jersey: Prentice-Hall, Inc., 1966), pp. 68–69, 76–78, 81–83, 90; Carl Thomas Devine, "Asset Cost and Expiration," *ibid.*, pp. 141–57; Raymond C. Dein, "Inventory Costs," *ibid.*, pp. 158–89; Norton Bedford, "Research, Selling, and Administrative Costs," *ibid.*, pp. 213–31; Michael Schiff, "Accounting Tactics and the Theory of the Firm," *Journal of Accounting Research*, IV (Spring, 1966), 62–63; and Robert R. Sterling, "Elements of Pure Accounting Theory," *Accounting Review*, XLII (January, 1967), 62–73.

[18] I argue this point in "The Amortization Problem: A Simplified Model and Some Unanswered Questions," *Journal of Accounting Research*, III (Spring, 1965), 104; compare A. C. Littleton, *Structure of Accounting Theory* (Madison, Wisconsin: American Accounting Association, 1953), p. 9; and Robert R. Sterling, "An Operational Analysis of Traditional Accounting," *Abacus*, II (December, 1966), 124. Other reasons for regarding inventories as similar to prepaid expenses and depreciable assets are given in Hendriksen (1965), pp. 246–47.

be associated with each of two or more periods.) Our previous discussion has concluded that *all* nonmonetary economic goods are part of the same continuum and subject to the same allocation problem, no matter how short the period from their acquisition to the point at which the accountant treats their services as exhausted.

The allocation problem

Except for unsold unlimited-life goods, all nonmonetary economic goods are allocated to the expenses or losses of one or more years—or to the acquisition prices of other nonmonetary goods acquired in one or more years. The allocation problem in financial accounting—and it is sufficiently pervasive and important to be called *the* allocation problem[19]—is to select and justify the particular allocation methods employed. This problem overlaps those which accountants traditionally have designated as problems of "cost accumulation" and of "matching costs with revenues."[20] These latter problems are among the most widespread and crucial in financial accounting.

As the Introduction asserts, given the present state of allocation theory it often will be impossible to give theoretical justification of the accountant's allocation methods, no matter which method he chooses. For simplicity, this will be demonstrated in detail for only one kind of nonmonetary economic good: depreciable assets. But (as we will see later) the arguments developed for depreciable assets are pertinent to *all* nonmonetary economic goods. Therefore, it will be argued that at present the accountant cannot justify his cost accumulation and matching efforts, no matter what methods he uses.

II. Theoretical Justification of Allocations[21]

"Theoretical justification" could mean various things. The issue of theoretical justification arises when the accountant wishes to prepare financial statements.[22] For

---

[19] This study is *not* directly concerned with such problems as the interperiod allocation of taxes, or the assignment of tax charges to individual projects (see Howard J. McBride, "Assigning Tax Loads to Prospective Projects," *Accounting Review*, XXXVIII [April, 1963], 363–70.) Nor is it concerned with cost accounting allocations, and the like. The author anticipates that many of the same considerations would apply to these problems as to the ones discussed here, but further research needs to be done. The allocation problem is also related to the general problem of assigning joint or common costs to different activities within an entity. Bows describes this problem well:

"Every diversified business of any size has joint costs for facilities, common personnel and overall financial resources which it uses in the various activities of its business as it sees fit. The most common joint costs are:

1. Financing costs, such as interest and preferred dividends
2. General and administrative expenses
3. Research and product development
4. Institutional advertising
5. Federal and other income taxes."

(Albert J. Bows, Jr., "Problems in Disclosure of Segments of Conglomerate Companies," *Journal of Accountancy*, CXXII [December, 1966], 35.) The conglomerate company problem discussed by Bows is a new and interesting one in financial accounting allocations. A similar problem may arise if federal regulatory agencies actively seek entity profit data by product lines.

[20] Grady (1965), pp. 74, 99–100; AAA (Matching), pp. 368–69. The term "allocation" is used rather than "cost accumulation" or "matching" because it has greater precision and corresponds better to language employed in economic theory.

[21] The section from here to the end of this chapter is crucial to the rest of this study. If the choice of requirements for theoretical justification of allocations has overlooked something, or otherwise erred, many subsequent conclusions collapse. Comments are invited. All that can be claimed is that I have tried to defend the requirements chosen, and to discuss as many alternative approaches as possible.

[22] Of course, the issue may also arise as an *abstract* question. For example, a philosopher might argue that anything that exists is justified—by the very fact that it exists:

any individual nonmonetary input, various different allocation methods may be available. If the accountant is to prepare a report, he must choose one, and only one, of these possible methods for each input. The problem of theoretical justification is one of defending his choice . . . . But there are several possible alternate criteria of what would *constitute* defense of an allocation method. It is essential for subsequent arguments to be as precise as possible here. In the remainder of this chapter, I try to discuss all of the different possibilities. It is demonstrated that most of the alternate criteria either are not germane to accounting, or are not germane to the particular accounting problems being examined in this book. But three of the possible criteria *are* pertinent. The following are minimum requirements for theoretical justification of an allocation method; these, and the various rejected alternate criteria, are discussed in detail below:

1. The method should be unambiguous.
2. It should be possible to defend the method. (Different possible ways of conducting such a defense are discussed below.)
3. The method should divide up what is available to be allocated, no more and no less. The allocation should be *additive*.

Later, the first and second requirements will be combined into:

It should be possible to specify, unambiguously and in advance, the method to be used, and defend that choice against all competing alternatives.

But this latter version must itself be defended. The discussion that follows is closely related to matters that are discussed in subsequent chapters. For this discussion to be efficient, it must at points summarize matters that later will be considered in more detail.[23] But it still will be possible to outline the main difficulties in justifying allocation methods.

Requirement 1: The method should be unambiguous

The first of these requirements is easily discussed. An allocation method should be unambiguous. It should yield an unique allocation. This is to say that the accountant should have made a clear-cut unequivocal choice of method. One should not be left undecided among a set of possible alternatives, each consistent with the accountant's decision, yet each leading to different allocation patterns. An allocation method should not leave one at a loss for how to allocate. Instead, it should provide clear instructions as to how the allocation should be conducted, and provide them *in advance* (theorists are seeking methods consistent with *general* justification—a method which had to be altered with the facts of each case would not be very satisfactory).

Margaret Fuller: "I accept the Universe!"

Thomas Carlyle: "Gad! she'd better."—See *Oxford Dictionary of Quotations*, 2nd Edition (Oxford: The Oxford University Press, 1955), s. v. "Carlyle."

But this leads to deeper waters than we need to plumb. The existence of abstract problems does not negate the existence of a concrete problem; the concrete problem of defending the accountant's choice must be faced regardless of whatever *other*, more abstract, problems may also exist. And it is this concrete problem with which this book is concerned.

[23] The problem faced here is that most of the concepts developed in this book are interrelated, yet one must begin discussing them one at a time. This means that it also is necessary in places (during the earlier chapters) to assert conclusions that will not be proven until later. I am intensely aware of the potential danger of circular argument that this creates, but believe that by the time the reader has completed Chapter Four it will be apparent that circularity has been avoided.

Requirement 2: It should be possible to defend the method

The second requirement, that the method be defensible, leads into deep waters. It will be demonstrated in the next chapter (using depreciation as an example) that accounting's allocations cannot be defended by the kinds of physical proofs that are possible in some of the sciences—that, for example, knowledge of the engineering characteristics of a machine is not sufficient to settle how that machine should be depreciated. Therefore, we must ask: how does one give theoretical justification to something that is not subject to physical demonstration?

It is generally accepted (and some believe it has been proved by Gödel[24]) that any theoretical structure must ultimately depend upon *some* assumptions or axioms which have not been given theoretical justification within that structure. And it has long been recognized that financial accounting requires such axioms:

> The fundamental concepts or propositions of accounting, like those of other fields, are in themselves assumptions in considerable measure or are predicated upon assumptions which are not subject to conclusive demonstration or proof.[25]

It would of course be ridiculous to claim that no theoretical structure can be given theoretical justification! Instead, the way in which a theoretical structure ordinarily is justified *despite* its need for axioms that cannot be justified within that structure is to appeal to some more general framework of thought—to look to a broader context in which there is a rule to which all parties agree, then demonstrate that the matter in question is a consequence of that general rule. (As an example, in discussing possible traffic controls for a residential area, one might argue that the framework in which traffic controls should be evaluated is merely one aspect of a broader framework in which decisions are evaluated in terms of their effects on general human welfare. Within this broader context, there is a general rule that preservation of children's lives takes priority over most other considerations. This rule could be cast in specific terms, then taken as an axiom of the traffic control discussion.)

This study is concerned with whether financial accounting's allocations can be theoretically justified, or whether they must inevitably be arbitrary. In discussing this, the broader appeal cannot be to what other *accountants* would agree to or believe.[26] That would be circular: "what other accountants believe" includes the very matters at issue.[27] So, the broader appeal must be to what *non*accountants believe.[28]

---

[24] For an unusually clear discussion of Gödel's conclusions, in layman's language, see Ernest Nagel and James R. Newman, "Gödel's Proof," *Scientific American*, CXCIV (June, 1956), 71–86.

[25] Paton and Littleton (1940), p. 21.

[26] Even were such an appeal legitimate, it would not suffice. A strong case can be made that the choice of particular allocation methods cannot be defended against alternative methods even from *within* the financial accounting system, except by arbitrary fiat. But this argument need not be presented in this study.

[27] This is not to say that the accountant's customary appeal to generally accepted accounting principles is *usually* circular, only that it would be circular *in this case*. Usually when this appeal is made the matter at issue is some particular accounting *practice*. But here the matter at issue is of fundamental importance to the generally accepted accounting principles *themselves*.

It is demonstrated in subsequent chapters that the way in which accountants perceive allocations, and their beliefs about allocations, are basic to much of the rest of their thinking about accounting—the effects of these beliefs are pervasive. In fact, by Chapter Six it becomes evident that if accountants' allocation methods *cannot* be given theoretical justification, then neither can the bulk of conventional accounting practice, nor most of the alternatives to conventional practice that have been proposed by theorists. But this conventional practice and these alternatives have conditioned and dominated what accountants would agree to and believe. Therefore, it is circular to appeal to what other accountants would agree to or believe *when one is questioning their basic approaches to allocation*.

[28] In more technical language, the problem is to insure that financial accounting's allocation theory is "bound-

(Of course, should an allocation method *violate* what accountants believe, it could not be considered part of any "generally accepted" system of accounting.) This appeal could be in either of two directions:

1. One might appeal to rules upon which intelligent laymen would agree, arguing that accounting rules should be consequences of propositions which readers of accounting reports would concede. In the traffic example, the appeal to the priority of preserving children's lives might end the discussion.

2. One might appeal to some other discipline in which allocation theory has been studied. For accounting, the relevant outside discipline is economics,[29] and economists *have* studied allocation carefully and at length.

Difficulties with these appeals

Unfortunately (to anticipate the conclusions of this study) both appeals lead to difficulties. When one tries to defend allocation methods, each appeal to a rule or a principle usually leads to another issue. Each answer usually leads to another question that, to the layman, is as sensible as the one before. It is difficult to defend allocation methods in ways that laymen would find *conclusive*, though such an attempt is discussed in Chapter Six.

The allocation theories developed by *economists* have been created for quite different kinds of problems than those that confront the accountant. Not only are there reasons to doubt that the economists' theories are adaptable to the accountants' problems, but it will be argued that typically the economists' theories are simply irrelevant to financial accounting's allocations.

The appeal to purpose

Several readers of earlier versions of this study have made what amounts to a reply to the previous comments. "The difficulties mentioned," they might say, "are consequences of discussing allocations *in the abstract*. The justification of any allocation method will depend on the purpose to be served. Once objectives, alternatives, and payoffs have been identified, there really should be no further difficulties with allocations." There are two main weaknesses to this position:

1. Presently, there is no unanimity about the purposes to be served by accounting, much less the purposes to be served by allocations. Nor, despite much effort by theorists, is there any sign that such agreement is near. To extent that the different goals give any guidance for allocation at all, they seem to lead to differing allocation methods that conflict with the accomplishment of other purposes.[30]

---

ed," i.e. that its primitive terms extend at least as far as other contexts, and are acceptable primitive terms in these contexts (or derivable from other primitive terms in those contexts).

One cannot eliminate *all* arbitrariness from a theoretical structure, because of the necessity of such primitive terms; attempts to do so lead to the dilemma of philosophical doubt reached by Descartes: nothing is known without *some* arbitrariness, except the bare experience of cognition. But for one's theoretical structure to be theoretically justified, its arbitrariness should be no greater than that found in adjacent contexts.

[29] This comment is applicable only to *present* financial accounting theory. As is pointed out in Chapter Six, much promising research is being done in relating financial accounting to such things as measurement science and the behavioral sciences. But none of this effort has yet reached the point where it allows a fully convincing appeal to be made.

[30] This can be seen readily enough for certain goals, such as obtaining the social or financial benefits of suppressing fluctuations in reported profits. But it is true in more subtle cases, too. The following is offered tentatively, and only as a possible example of the difficulties one can experience using this approach.

Suppose that we perceive company profit maximization by management as the purpose to be served by accounting. Allocation in terms of a good's marginal net-revenue contributions (discussed in the next chapter)

[handwritten marginalia: Why don't you state what you think the good goals of acct are so this could be done?]

What is needed is general agreement on a priority of financial accounting goals. Should such agreement eventually be reached, it *might* lead to conclusive ways to justify allocation methods in accounting. But there is no such general agreement yet, and it must be realized that whatever may happen eventually is no help in justifying allocation methods *now*.

2. Even were agreement reached on the purpose of accounting, it does not follow that our first requirement for justifying allocation methods (that the method be unambiguous) would be met. Most of the purposes proposed for accounting in recent years seem consistent with a great *variety* of possible allocation methods. The truth of this observation is obvious when the proposed purpose is broad and unspecific (for example, for such broad criteria as *fairness* or *relevance*). But it is equally true of more detailed statements of purpose, such as those in the recent AAA "Basic Theory" statement, or Grady's Inventory.[31]

Accounting is an artifact. The purpose of any artifact depends on the purposes of its users. Whatever the purpose of financial accounting may eventually be agreed on to be, presumably that purpose will be a *derived* one that depends on the purposes of some or all of the readers of financial statements. Much of the allocation problem in financial accounting results from the present dearth of a rigorous theory of relating allocation methods to reader purposes (and a lack of rigorous theory about such things as appropriate reader decision models).

All of these are negative conclusions, and therefore hard to support in detail except by a very inefficient process of elimination. Instead, the reader is invited to provide counter-examples. Specifically, the reader is challenged to read the rest of this study, then specify a serious purpose for financial accounting that stands a reasonable chance of gaining general acceptance, and provides unambiguous guidance in, say, the choice of depreciation and inventory allocation methods.

Certain highly specialized purposes, such as those of tax or regulatory accounting, may provide such unambiguous guidance. But these are not appropriate for general financial accounting. Chapter Six discusses two approaches to accounting that *avoid* the allocation problem by *refusing to make* allocations of nonmonetary goods,[32] but that is another matter entirely.

Paralleling my earlier remarks, future research may lead to development of a generally accepted purpose for financial accounting that provides unambiguous guidance in the choice of allocation methods. But there does not seem to be any such purpose available *now*, and once again the appeal to purpose is irrelevant.

"Satisficing" justifications

The present failure of the appeal to purpose results in the failure of another possible approach to theoretical justification of allocation methods. One might argue that it is

seems a natural consequence of using marginal contributions analysis for management's decisions. Costs determined in this way are highly relevant for managerial profit-maximizing purposes. But there is no reason to believe that these figures also are relevant to the decision processes of readers of financial statements. The figures are relevant to decisions concerning resource allocation within the firm. They are at best only tangentially relevant to, say, the stockholder's decision of whether to buy, hold, or sell shares of common stock—indeed, in Chapter Three arguments are advanced that they are *irrelevant* to such decisions.

[31] Committee to Prepare a Statement of Basic Accounting Theory, *A Statement of Basic Accounting Theory* (Evanston, Illinois: American Accounting Association, 1966), *passim*; Grady (1965), pp. 56–67, 73; see also Kohler (1963), pp. 10–11, 212; and Hendriksen (1965), pp. 81–83.

[32] Somewhat simplified forms of the current-price approaches recommended by Chambers and Sterling, and a net-quick-assets version of the cash-flow approaches recommended by some financial analysts.

unnecessary to demonstrate that a particular allocation method is better than all possible alternatives—that it is enough that the method be a satisfactory one. But satisfactory for *what*? Presumably for whatever purposes are to be served by the allocation.

One always can assert that for one's *own* purposes a particular allocation method is satisfactory. This is a psychological statement—at least in part. Therefore, it may be impossible to challenge its truth. However, at most it gives only a personal, private, theoretical justification to the allocation method—one which does not necessarily pertain to anyone else.[33] But theorists have been seeking to give *general* theoretical justifications to allocation methods. Lacking any general agreement about purpose, the satisficer is left in the awkward position of having to demonstrate that his method is satisfactory for all purposes. The literature of accounting controversy (of which a number of examples are cited in this study) suggests that such demonstrations are impossible. Usually, only trivial rules satisfy all goals.

Besides, there is another problem. Once one is willing to assert that various conflicting methods all are satisfactory, one also is willing (by implication) to ignore whatever differences in the reported figures result from choosing one method rather than another.[34] In effect one is satisfied with bias in one's allocations, so long as the bias does not exceed the difference between the results of those satisfactory allocation methods whose results conflict the most. Chapter Six will argue that, except under fairly rigid conditions, the amount of bias involved will often be more than is satisfactory to many readers of financial statements. When this is true, the "satisficing" method once again fails of general theoretical justification.

Surrogates and materiality

It is not unusual for theory to indicate that a particular approach to a problem is desirable, yet for that approach to be barred by practical considerations. (For example, in the next chapter we will see that several theorists believe this is true of discounted-contributions, or "economic" valuation of assets.) Under such circumstances it can be quite justifiable to employ some surrogate approach that *is* practical.

But the use of surrogates does not allow one to avoid the underlying problem of justifying the allocation method that was chosen as being theoretically correct. Much the same can be said of approximations made for convenience and other matters falling under the heading of materiality—such as assertions that various different methods are satisfactory because they all differ insignificantly from the theoretically correct method. If one could determine that a complex monotonic decreasing function was appropriate for depreciating an asset, it might be appropriate to approximate it with a simple linear function. But if one wishes to give theoretical justification to depreciation allocations, the appropriateness of the original complex function must be defended.[35] And if such a defense cannot be provided, that failure is not merely a

---

[33] A case could be made that, instead of being a psychological statement, this is an assertion that the method satisfies certain subjectively defined ends. The result would still be personal, rather than general, theoretical justification.

[34] As an example, suppose that someone has two exterior thermometers on his house, and that they give readings as much as five degrees apart. If he is indifferent to which thermometer he looks at, then he is indifferent to a five degree difference in reported temperature.

[35] The reader is invited to compare this discussion with that in Wixon and Kell (1960), p. (12-4); and Raymond J. Chambers, *Accounting, Evaluation and Economic Behavior* (Englewood Cliffs, New Jersey: Prentice-Hall, Inc., 1966), pp. 229–31, 260–61.

matter of *employing an approximation.* (Similarly, the use of accelerated depreciation to compensate for inflation implies that otherwise some depreciation pattern closer to straight-line would have been appropriate; rules of thumb imply defensibility as adequate replacements to theoretically justified solutions that we did not have the time to calculate; and so forth.)

Surrogates are an appropriate response to lack of data, but *not* to a lack of theory: for convenience, this study will assume throughout most of its arguments that there *are* no data problems. This is not because data problems are not serious, but because we are going to examine more fundamental difficulties. So the question of surrogates will not arise.[36] Similarly, since the points discussed in this study are mainly theoretical ones, the issue of materiality is not vital.

Summary

We may now combine the first two requirements. If an allocation method is to be theoretically justified, it should be possible to specify unambiguously and in advance the method to be used, and to defend that choice against all competing alternatives. At present, whatever approach one adopts to financial accounting, there usually will be a variety of conflicting methods, all of which seem consistent with what one is trying to accomplish: the allocation problem often is one of an embarrassment of riches. Further research may provide better answers. But, as subsequent chapters will demonstrate, at present there seems no way to defend our choices conclusively.

Partial defenses

All of this relates to a point that will become quite important in the next chapter. Often an accountant who wishes to employ a particular allocation method will give a *partial* defense of it. Anticipating an example that will be used later, an accountant might try to justify straight-line depreciation of a machine by arguing that he expects the machine to be run an equal number of hours each year. But if he stops here his defense of straight-line depreciation is incomplete. For one could ask: why should an equal portion of the machine's acquisition price be allocated to each hour?

Perhaps the machine produces more in the early years than it will later. Or perhaps its output will command a higher price in the early years. In either case some declining-charge method might be more appropriate. In the next chapter we will examine this kind of problem in more detail. For the present, the point to be emphasized is that if one is going to give theoretical justification to what one does, *all* implicit decisions must be justified (in the sense of "justification" given earlier in this section), not just some of them. Otherwise there always will be *some* conflicting alternative against which one has no defense, holes in one's reasoning allowing mutually inconsistent methods to be equally acceptable, with no conclusive way of *settling* the conflict. Some method or other *will* be chosen, of course. But the choice will be arbitrary.

It should be repeated that there are limits to how far an allocation method need be

---

[36] Otherwise, we would make extensive use of the discussion of attributes of a satisfactory surrogate in Yuji Ijiri, Robert K. Jaedicke, and Kenneth E. Knight, "The Effects of Accounting Alternatives on Management Decisions," in Robert K. Jaedicke, Yuji Ijiri, and Oswald Nielsen, editors, *Research in Accounting Measurement* (Evanston, Illinois: American Accounting Association, 1966), pp. 188–92. The discussion on page 189 is particularly relevant to some of the remarks made previously in this chapter. A "satisfactory" surrogate is satisfactory with respect to a particular decision, a particular purpose. But we have seen that in financial accounting the purposes are varied and conflicting, with no way at present to set priorities.

defended. If the method chosen can be defended by an appeal to rules upon which intelligent laymen would agree, or by an appeal to economists' theories of allocation, the justification may suffice. It also should be observed that there is nothing necessarily wrong with arbitrary methods. Most of us chose our wives by methods that at various crucial points were indifferent to theory. Many successful business decisions are made without full theoretical defense; sometimes this is what is involved when we say that a decision has been influenced by considerations that cannot be quantified, or that a decision required expert judgment. But if an allocation method is to be theoretically justified, it must be defended completely, in the sense indicated above. Lacking a complete defense, the choice of method inevitably is arbitrary.

Decisions under ignorance

Certain other disciplines have tried to develop ways to deal with situations similar to those to which accountants respond with partial defenses—ways to give theoretical justification to decisions when no explicit way to defend one's choices is known. An example is Bernoulli's principle of attaching equal probabilities to future events when one has no idea of which events might materialize.[37] It can be argued that such rules for behavior in the face of ignorance are justified (in a theory of uncertainty) when decisions must be made despite incomplete knowledge. However, such rules do not seem pertinent to this discussion.

1. Whether accountants *must* make allocation decisions is a major question under examination in this study. Chapter Six advances reasons why accountants should *not* make allocations, thereby eliminating a large part of the justification for rules of behavior under ignorance.

2. Much of the theory of appropriate behavior under ignorance pertains to cases in which the ignorance arises from lack of data—data which, if available, would support a decision. Here, the problem turns out to be much more serious: lack of a theory to justify one's allocation methods, *no matter what data are available.* (This point is developed in Chapters Three through Six.)

3. In any case, accountants do not at present have any systematic theory of appropriate behavior under ignorance. Similarly, they lack any theoretically justified way of ranking arbitrariness—of saying "this kind of arbitrariness is preferable to that kind"—except as a psychological (or subjective) statement with which others may agree, but just as well may not agree. Once again future research may provide what is presently lacking, but no such theory exists *now* to justify our allocation methods.

Requirement 3: The method should divide up what is available to be allocated

The first two minimum criteria for theoretical justification of an allocation method —unambiguity and defensibility—have now been discussed. The third requirement for theoretical justification of an allocation method is that it should *allocate:* should divide up what there is to be divided, no more and no less. There is nothing subtle about this requirement. There are various ways to divide a pie among three people. But it is clear from the outset that an allocation method that requires each person to

---

[37] Or any of the alternative strategies that have been recommended—for example, see Robert Schlaifer, *Probability and Statistics for Business Decisions* (New York: McGraw-Hill Book Company, Inc., 1959), pp. 445–46.

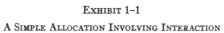

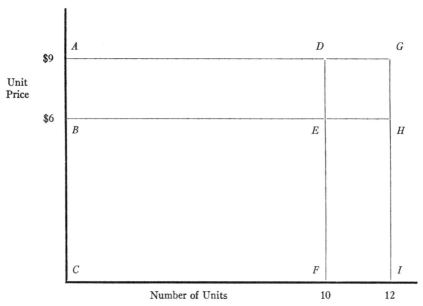

receive half the pie cannot be justified. If one is trying to dispose of the entire pie, a method that requires each person to receive one quarter of the pie cannot be justified, either.[38]

Consider an artificial example from elementary cost accounting.[39] Suppose that product standards specify that 10 units of raw material costing $6 per unit shall be used in manufacturing one unit of product. Instead, 12 units are used at a cost of $9 per unit. Exhibit 1-1 is the usual diagram provided for such cases.

The total cost of raw material used was $12 \times \$9 = \$108$. In an elementary discussion of variance accounting, this $108 would be allocated as follows:

Number of units used

	Rectangle	Amount
To the acquisition price.................	*BEFC*	$ 60
To a price variance.....................	*AGHB*	36
To a quantity variance.................	*EHIF*	12
Total............................	*AGIC*	$108

Consider the price variance, *AGHB*. This is made up of two components: a "pure"

---

[38] Devine argues that there are cases in accounting where it is unnecessary that the amounts allocated add up to the total amount to be allocated. But he is speaking of situations in which different measurement conventions are applied to the whole and to the parts, something which we will take care to avoid in what follows. See Devine (1962), pp. 205–206.

[39] No departure from the emphasis on financial accounting should be inferred from this use of a cost accounting example; it is employed merely because it is simple, familiar, and clear-cut. Examples from financial accounting will be discussed later in this study.

price variance ($ADEB=\$30$) and an *interaction* variance ($DGHE=\$6$). This interaction variance is a *joint* result of too much usage at too high a price. In elementary cost accounting this interaction variance is added to the "pure" price variance, for reasons that need not concern us here. The point to recognize is that cost accounting theory does not ignore the interaction variance.

Interactions will be present in accounting whenever the effects of different factors are not independent. Ordinarily, we would expect the firm's nonmonetary goods to interact. If these inputs *are* independent (if, for example, the total receipts earned by the firm are not greater than what the individual inputs would have earned alone) the company should consider liquidating. It will be argued in Chapter Three that these interaction effects are substantial. To be theoretically justified, an allocation method cannot just pretend that interaction effects do not exist. In a similar context (later extended to include the kinds of cases discussed in this study) Gould points out the logical fallacy in allocations that "attempt to treat B as independent of A when the conditions of the problem state that A and B are interdependent."[40]

Summary

The minimum requirements for giving theoretical justification to an allocation method are that it should be possible to specify, unambiguously and in advance, the method to be used, and to defend that choice against all competing alternatives—and that the method should divide up what there is to allocate, no more and no less. We have seen that appropriate defenses for allocation methods may be found in what laymen would agree to, or in allocation theories developed by economists. Several other possible appeals have been examined, but found to be of no present help. During this study several more possible ways of justifying allocation methods will be examined.

The discussion indicated that there are several areas in which further research might help in justifying allocation methods. It would be very valuable were general agreement reached on the priority of accounting goals, and were goals selected that had unambiguous implications for the choice of allocation methods; it also would be valuable were a theory of appropriate behavior under ignorance developed for accounting. During this study several more areas in which valuable research might be performed will be mentioned.

Finally, theoretical justification of an allocation method requires defense of *all* its implicit assumptions, up to the limits set by an appeal to economic theory or the rules followed by intelligent laymen. However, there is nothing necessarily wrong with arbitrary allocations—so long as one does not treat them as being theoretically justified.

---

[40] J. R. Gould, "The Economist's Cost Concept and Business Problems," in W. T. Baxter and Sidney Davidson, editors, *Studies in Accounting Theory* (Homewood, Illinois: Richard D. Irwin, Inc., 1962), p. 231.

CHAPTER TWO

Present Approaches to Depreciation

Because of the significant effects on financial position and results of operations of the depreciation method or methods used, the following disclosures should be made in the financial statements or in notes thereto:

a. Depreciation expense for the period,

b. Balances of major classes of depreciable assets, by nature or function, at the balance-sheet date,

c. Accumulated depreciation, either by major classes of depreciable assets or in total, at the balance-sheet date, and

d. A general description of the method or methods used in computing depreciation with respect to major classes of depreciable assets.[1]

Depreciation is probably the most discussed and most disputatious topic in all accounting.[2]

I WILL discuss the allocation problem in financial accounting by examining what most would agree is a particularly severe instance of it: the ways in which accountants depreciate depreciable assets.[3] Present accounting literature suggests five main approaches to calculating depreciation (along with several minor approaches mentioned briefly in what follows).[4] In effect, though, only two of these approaches are used in present financial accounting practice.

---

[1] Accounting Principles Board, "APB Opinion No. 12: Omnibus Opinion—1967," *Journal of Accountancy* CXXV (February, 1968), 55.

[2] Sidney Davidson, "Depreciation, Income Taxes, and Growth," *Accounting Research*, VIII (July, 1957), 191.

[3] The following are good references for the sense in which depreciation is a kind of allocation process:

"*Depreciation accounting* is a system of accounting which aims to distribute the cost or other basic value of tangible capital assets, less salvage (if any), over the estimated useful life of the unit . . . It is a process of allocation, not of valuation. *Depreciation for the year* is the portion of the total charge under such a system that is allocated to the year."

—Accounting Terminology Bulletin Number 1, in *Accounting Research and Terminology Bulletins*, Final Edition (New York: American Institute of Certified Public Accountants, 1961), p. 25.

"The problem is to decide how much of the cost of the asset will be charged to several periods so the entire cost may be allocated to the periods in which the asset is used productively."

—Harold Bierman, Jr., "Depreciable Assets—Timing of Expense Recognition," *Accounting Review*, XXXVI (October, 1961), 613. Storey has described the decision to treat accounting as an allocation process (and the corresponding rejection of accounting as a valuation process) as the "fundamental axiom" upon which much of modern accounting theory is based—see Reed K. Storey, "Accounting Principles: AAA and AICPA," *Journal of Accountancy*, CXVII (June, 1964), 49–50. See also Rufus Wixon and Walter G. Kell, editors, *Accountants' Handbook* (New York: The Ronald Press Company, 1960), p. (17–1); Robert T. Sprouse and Maurice Moonitz, *A Tentative Set of Broad Accounting Principles for Business Enterprises*, Accounting Research Study No. 3 (New York: American Institute of Certified Public Accountants, 1962), pp. 34, 58; Eric L. Kohler, *A Dictionary for Accountants*, Third Edition (Englewood Cliffs, New Jersey: Prentice-Hall, Inc., 1963), p. 14; and Paul Grady, *Inventory of Generally Accepted Accounting Principles for Business Enterprises*, Accounting Research Study No. 7 (New York: American Institute of Certified Public Accountants, 1965), pp. 100–101, 126, 148–51.

[4] This chapter again asks that the reader verify for himself that the observations made are fair. As in Chapter One, the matters at issue are not ones that can be settled merely by appeals to authority. The following sources are offered only as general background. References to specific points will be given later, where appropriate. For bibliographical material (some of which is repeated below), see Eldon S. Hendriksen, *Accounting Theory* (Homewood, Illinois: Richard D. Irwin, Inc., 1965) pp. 220–21, 304–305, 334–35. See also Wixon and Kell (1960), Chapters 16 and 17; Sprouse and Moonitz (1962), Chapters 3 and 4; Kohler (1963), various entries; Grady (1965), Chapter 4; Hendriksen (1965), Chapters 8, 11, 12; the following reports of committees of the American Account-

Demonstration of this is made easier by using an example. Suppose that at the start of Year 1 a company buys a machine for $1,100. For simplicity, assume that the machine has a zero estimated scrap value upon retirement, and that it will not be used to manufacture an inventory.[5] Suppose that the accountant decides to depreciate the machine according to the following pattern:

Year 1	$ 400
Year 2	400
Year 3	300
Total	$1,100

The accountant intends that these amounts will form part of the total expenses reported on the company's income statements for Years 1, 2, and 3. How did he go about determining this particular depreciation pattern? The subsequent discussion will be confined to approaches actively discussed in the accounting literature[6]—for instance, certain engineering approaches to depreciation will be mostly ignored (for reasons that will be explained later).[7] Even so, there are several main ways in which the accountant might have obtained this depreciation pattern. The first three involve allocations of historical acquisition prices; the latter two are valuation approaches.

ing Association: "Accounting and Reporting Standards for Corporate Financial Statements—1957 Revision," *Accounting Review* XXXII (October, 1957), 536–46; "Accounting for Land, Buildings, and Equipment," *Accounting Review*, XXXIX (July, 1964), 693–99; "A Discussion of Various Approaches to Inventory Measurement," *Accounting Review*, XXXIX (July, 1964), 700–14; "The Realization Concept," *Accounting Review*, XL (April, 1965), 312–22; "The Matching Concept," *Accounting Review*, XL (April, 1965), 368–72; *A Statement of Basic Accounting Theory* (Evanston, Illinois: American Accounting Association, 1966). See also William A. Paton and A. C. Littleton, *An Introduction to Corporate Accounting Standards* (Columbus, Ohio: American Accounting Association, 1940), pp. 81–85, 88–89; Eugene L. Grant and Paul T. Norton, Jr., *Depreciation*, Revised Printing (New York: The Ronald Press Company, 1955), *passim*; Oscar S. Gellein, "The Decreasing-Charge Concept," *Journal of Accountancy*, C (August, 1955), 56–61; Lewis A. Carman, "Non-Linear Depreciation," *Accounting Review*, XXXI (July, 1956), 454–91; Frank A. Singer, "Depreciation'—Better Left Unsaid," *Accounting Review*, XXXII (July, 1957), 406–12; Willard J. Graham, "Depreciation and Capital Replacement in an Inflationary Economy," *Accounting Review*, XXXIV (July, 1959), 367–75; Edgar O. Edwards and Philip W. Bell, *The Theory and Measurement of Business Income* (Berkeley: University of California Press, 1961), 161–88; L. Goldberg, "Concepts of Depreciation," in W. T. Baxter and Sidney Davidson, editors, *Studies in Accounting Theory* (Homewood, Illinois: Richard D. Irwin, Inc., 1962), pp. 236–58; G. J. Ponsonby, "Depreciation With Special Reference to Transport," *ibid.*, pp. 259–70; Carl Thomas Devine, *Essays in Accounting Theory* (privately printed, 1962), II, pp. 241–70, 338–41; Norton M. Bedford, *Income Determination Theory: An Accounting Framework* (Reading, Massachusetts: Addison-Wesley Publishing Company, Inc., 1965), Chapter 8; Harold Bierman, Jr., *Financial Accounting Theory* (New York: The Macmillan Company, 1965), pp. 112–22; Curtis Holt Stanley, *Objectivity in Accounting* (Ann Arbor, Michigan: The University of Michigan, 1965), pp. 61–65; F. K. Wright, "Depreciation and Obsolescence in Current Value Accounting," *Journal of Accounting Research*, III (Autumn, 1965), 167–81; M. C. Wells, "A Note on the Amortization of Fixed Assets," *Accounting Review*, XLIII (April, 1968), 373–76 Finally, see David Green, Jr., and George H. Sorter, "Accounting for Obsolescence—A Proposal," *Accounting Review*, XXXIV (July, 1959), 433–41; Harold Bierman, Jr., "Recording Obsolescence," *Journal of Accounting Research*, II (Autumn, 1964), 229–35; and J. H. Woods, "Recording Obsolescence: A Note," *Journal of Accounting Research*, III (Autumn, 1965), 261–63.

[5] For additional simplicity, the examples in this study all involve goods whose total service lives are assumed to be known in advance (and known correctly). Having made this implicit assumption, the depreciation problem becomes one of different possible patterns of allocation to a single set of service years. Of course, much of the actual variability in depreciation patterns results from different possible estimates in *service lives*. For an interesting example, see Allan R. Drebin, "'Cash-Flowitis': Malady or Syndrome?" *Journal of Accounting Research*, II (Spring, 1964), 27–29.

[6] A good introduction to the variety of approaches actually used is Kohler (1963), pp. 176–82.

[7] Sosnick's offsetting-interest method is also temporarily ignored; it will be discussed in Chapter Five, at which point the method's implicit assumptions may be examined more efficiently. See Stephen H. Sosnick, "Depreciation: The Offsetting-Interest Method," *Accounting Review*, XXXVII (January, 1962), 59–66.

$\left\{ \begin{array}{l} \text{1. Arbitrary approaches} \\ \text{2. Net-revenue-contributions approaches} \\ \text{3. Other-services approaches} \\ \text{4. Discounted-contributions valuation approach} \\ \text{5. Current-price valuation approaches.} \end{array} \right.$

1. Arbitrary approaches

Perhaps the accountant is following some arbitrary way of allocating the $1,100 acquisition price to the three income statements—"arbitrary" in the sense of "not theoretically justified" discussed in the previous chapter. Perhaps, instead of puzzling out how the machine *should* be depreciated, he has just used some standard formula. For instance, perhaps he has used straight-line depreciation (over a 2-3/4 year estimated service life) because the method is easy to calculate and acceptable to his auditor. Or perhaps the accountant is allocating the $1,100 acquisition price to the three income statements in terms of something that has nothing directly to do with determining net income, but which concerns some other purpose. For instance, perhaps the depreciation pattern represents the way in which the accountant plans to write the machine off for tax purposes (yet the accountant does not believe that taxable income is necessarily the best possible measure of net income).

2. Net-revenue-contributions approaches[8]

The "net-revenue contributions" of a machine will be defined as the series of revenues or cost savings resulting from the firm's acquiring the machine, less whatever

[8] For examples of the following approach, see Grady (1965), pp. 99–102; Hendriksen (1965), pp. 312–13, 321–22, 325–32; Edwards and Bell (1961), pp. 176–83; and Carl Thomas Devine, "Asset Cost and Expiration," in Morton Backer, editor, *Modern Accounting Theory* (Englewood Cliffs, New Jersey: Prentice-Hall, Inc., 1966), p. 150.

The net-revenue-contributions approach to depreciation has become very important in recent accounting theory. Its evolution (and the forms of it used by theorists) are reflected in the works listed below. There are close links between the net-revenue-contributions approach and what below is called "discounted-contributions valuation" (economic valuation); any history of the one must in part be a history of the other. Indeed, some authors fail to distinguish sharply between the two approaches (especially when discussing income determination under certainty). The necessary distinctions will be emphasized later; meanwhile, the following works include several examples of discounted-contributions valuation.

See Richard P. Brief, "A Late Nineteenth Century Contribution to the Theory of Depreciation," *Journal of Accounting Research*, V (Spring, 1967), 27–38; J. D. Campbell, "Straight-Line Method of Depreciation," *Accounting Review*, XXVI (January, 1951), 40–42; Maurice Moonitz and Charles C. Staehling, *Accounting—An Analysis of Its Problems* (Brooklyn, New York: The Foundation Press, Inc., 1952), Volume 1, Chapter 5 (this chapter is the basis for Chapter 5 of Volume 1 of Maurice Moonitz and Louis H. Jordan, *Accounting—An Analysis of Its Problems*, Revised Edition [New York: Holt, Rinehart and Winston, Inc., 1963]); Ralph Coughenour Jones, *Effects of Price Level Changes on Business Income, Capital, and Taxes* (Urbana, Illinois: American Accounting Association, 1956), pp. 106–13; Hector R. Anton, "Depreciation, Cost Allocation and Investment Decisions," *Accounting Research*, VII (April, 1956), 117–34; John Coughlan, "Industrial Accounting," *Accounting Review*, XXXIV (July, 1959), 415–28 (it is not immediately evident, but this article *is* recommending a simple variant of the net-revenue-contributions approach; the reader who wishes to verify this should note that Coughlan used continuous compounding); Reed K. Storey, "Cash Movements and Periodic Income Determination," *Accounting Review*, XXXV (July, 1960), 449–54; Isaac N. Reynolds, "Selecting the Proper Depreciation Method," *Accounting Review*, XXXVI (April, 1961), 239–48; Bierman (1961); F. K. Wright, "Depreciation Theory and the Cost of Funds," *Accounting Review*, XXXVIII (January, 1963), 87–90; Howard D. Lowe, "The Essentials of a General Theory of Depreciation," *Accounting Review*, XXXVIII (April, 1963), 293–301; F. K. Wright, "Towards a General Theory of Depreciation," *Journal of Accounting Research*, II (Spring, 1964), 80–90, and *erratum*, III (Spring, 1965), p. 166; Bedford (1965), pp. 135–39; Bierman (1965), pp. 122–34; Ezra Solomon, "Return on Investment: The Relation of Book-Yield to True Yield," in Robert K. Jaedicke, Yuji Ijiri, and Oswald Nielsen, editors, *Research in Accounting Measurement* (Evanston, Illinois: American Accounting Association, 1966), pp. 232–44; Harold Bierman, Jr., "A Further Study of Depreciation," *Accounting Review*, XLI (April, 1966), 271–74; William A. Peterson, "Significance of Prospective Income Data," *Accounting Review*, XLI (April, 1966),

should be allocated to other inputs that may be required in generating that series. This is a *very* rough definition. It will be refined at the start of the next chapter, but it suffices for now.

Perhaps the accountant has estimated the pattern of the machine's effects on the firm's net revenues (over the machine's service life), and is allocating the $1,100 acquisition price according to this estimated pattern. Or, equivalently, perhaps the accountant has estimated a pattern of net cost savings resulting from acquisition of the machine, and is allocating the $1,100 acquisition price according to *this* pattern. For simplicity, the examples that follow will ignore the latter possibility, and speak only of net-revenue contributions. This is because revenues and cost savings have identical effects on the kinds of calculations involved.[9]

For example, suppose that the company expects the following increases in net revenues to result from acquiring the machine:

Year 1................. $510
Year 2.................   470
Year 3.................   330

As Table 2-1 demonstrates, this stream of estimated net-revenue contributions yields the company a 10 percent average rate of return on its investment. Therefore, 10 percent is the implicit earnings rate on the investment in this good by this firm. There is only one depreciation pattern that both:

1. Is consistent with this machine's acquisition price and estimated net-revenue contributions, *and*

2. Results in reporting the implicit (10 percent) rate of return on the investment in the machine during *each* year it is owned (assuming, of course, that things work out exactly as planned).[10] Table 2-2 shows one way to calculate this depreciation pattern.[11]

275–82; Allan R. Drebin, "Accounting for Proprietary Research," *Accounting Review*, XLI (July, 1966), 413–25; William J. Vatter, "Income Models, Book Yield, and the Rate of Return," *Accounting Review*, XLI (October, 1966), 681–98; T. N. Young and C. G. Peirson, "Depreciation—Future Services Basis," *Accounting Review*, XLII (April, 1967), 338–41 (the authors use simple instead of compound interest); F. K. Wright, "An Evaluation of Ladelle's Theory of Depreciation," *Journal of Accounting Research*, V (Autumn, 1967) pp. 173–79; Richard P. Brief and Joel Owen, "Depreciation and Capital Gains: A 'New' Approach," *Accounting Review*, XLIII (April, 1968) pp. 367–72; Richard P. Brief, "Depreciation Theory and Capital Gains," *Journal of Accounting Research*, VI (Spring, 1968), 149–52; and Orace Johnson, "Two General Concepts of Depreciation," *Journal of Accounting Research*, VI (Spring, 1968), 29–37.

[9] This is because they both increase net income—and increases and decreases in net income are what the calculations are sensitive to, not revenues and cost savings *per se*. The reason for discussing this approach in terms of effects on net income (instead of on cash flows) is that this is the way the income statement itself is constructed. See Bierman (1966) for the full argument. Of course, the two ways of discussing things can be reconciled; any reader who prefers to place a cash-flow interpretation on what is said is invited to do so. In fact, later on this study will speak in terms of cash flows, too, where cash flows seem the more appropriate concept.

In the following illustrations it is assumed that net-revenue-contributions occur at the ends of years, rather than continuously. Discrete compounding is also assumed. This is merely to make the computations easier. While this simplification does not affect the *theoretical* arguments employed, Luneski has presented arguments suggesting that this simplification can be a source of erroneous decisions in practical situations. See Chris J. Luneski, "Continuous Versus Discrete Compounding for Capital Budgeting Decisions," *Accounting Review*, XLII (October, 1967), 767–71.

Similarly, the "investment" in depreciable assets will be perceived as the beginning-of-year book value, rather than some average book value for the year. Taxes will be consistently ignored throughout this study—again, merely for simplicity. The reason for speaking of *average* rates of return is discussed in Chapter Five.

Readers unfamiliar with the kinds of capital budgeting calculations that underlie the tables in this chapter are referred to Harold Bierman, Jr., and Seymour Smidt, *The Capital Budgeting Decision*, Second Edition (New York: The Macmillan Company, 1966), Chapters 1–4.

[10] This is easily proved. Imagine a machine with a service life of N years and an acquisition price of K_1. Let Y_1, $Y_2, \ldots Y_N$ represent the net-revenue contributions of this machine in Years 1 through N. Suppose that the im-

TABLE 2-1

AN INVESTMENT WITH A 10% AVERAGE RATE OF RETURN

Year	Average Rate of Return	Appropriate Discount Factor	Estimated Net-Revenue Contributions	Present Value
1..............	10%	0.9091	$510	$ 464
2.............	10%	0.8264	470	388
3.............	10%	0.7513	330	248
Total...				.$1,100

TABLE 2-2

CALCULATION OF ANNUAL DEPRECIATION
FOR AN INVESTMENT WITH A 10% AVERAGE RATE OF RETURN
(DEPRECIATION PATTERN CHOSEN TO RESULT IN A 10% RATE OF RETURN FOR EACH YEAR)

Year	(A) Current Year Rate of Return	(B) Investment (Beginning-of-Year Book Value)	(C) Appropriate Earnings for Year $(A \times B)$	(D) Estimated Net-Revenue Contributions	Depreciation for the Year $(D-C)$
1........	10%	$1,100	$110	$510	$400
2........	10%	700	70	470	400
3........	10%	300	30	330	300

The company would not purchase the machine unless the present value of the machine's estimated net-revenue contributions equalled its purchase price at *some* positive implicit rate of return.[12] As long as the net-revenue contributions in each year are positive, it will always be possible to calculate a depreciation pattern in this way.

plicit rate of return on this investment is r. Let $D_1, D_2, \ldots D_N$ represent the annual depreciation charges in Years 1 through N.

During Year 1 the investment in the machine is K_1. An r percent rate of return on the firm's investment therefore will equal rK_1. Since the net-revenue contributions for the year are Y_1, the following must be true if a return of rK_1 is to be reported for the year:

$$Y_1 - D_1 = rK_1$$

—from which it follows that $D_1 = Y_1 - rK_1$. During Year 2, the investment in the machine is:

$$K_1 - D_1 = K_1 - (Y_1 - rK_1) = (1 + r)K_1 - Y_1 = K_2$$

By the same logic,

$$D_2 = Y_2 - rK_2$$

In general, in Year h $(1 \leq h \leq n)$, $D_h = Y_h - rK_h$. Therefore, there is a unique depreciation charge for each year, consistent with the machine's acquisition price, its estimated pattern of net-revenue contributions, and with reporting an r percent rate of return each year on the investment in the machine. Compare Edwards and Bell (1961), p. 176.

For use of the implicit rate of return in this manner, see Reynolds (1961), p. 244. Another way to interpret the net-revenue-contributions approach is that if the $1,100 were borrowed there would be only one repayment pattern consistent with the estimated net-revenue contributions that resulted in a 10 percent interest rate being paid on the unpaid balance of the debt during each year that the debt was outstanding. Under the net-revenue contributions approach, the depreciation pattern is made to coincide with this repayment plan.

[11] This table is modeled after one used by Vatter in his discussion of this approach. See Vatter (1966), pp. 691-98.

[12] Under some circumstances, more than one positive implicit rate of return will be associated with a particular set of net-revenue contributions and acquisition price. Such multiple-yield cases are discussed in the Appendix to this chapter.

Call this the *"net-revenue-contributions approach"* to depreciation. The details of the allocations involved here are discussed at the beginning of the next chapter. As Chapter Five will indicate, this is not the only possible kind of net-revenue-contributions model. For example, it is possible to allocate in terms of net-revenue contributions without worrying about rates of return. However (as will be demonstrated) the same conclusions apply to all such variants of the net-revenue-contributions method as do to the forms of that method discussed here. Two things should be pointed out about this approach:

1. It is a way of allocating historical cost, *not* a valuation approach (although it does depend on valuation of the estimated net-revenue contributions for its allocation scheme). The comparable valuation approaches will be discussed shortly.[13] The net-revenue-contributions approach to depreciation is merely a way of matching the historical acquisition price of an asset with the net revenues or cost savings that it is expected to generate. As Young and Peirson comment (using "internal rate" where I have used "implicit rate"), "the use of the internal rate of earnings implies that the total amount to be allocated as depreciation is the historical cost of the asset."[14]

2. In practice, this approach is often applied in much broader, less precise, ways than have been used here. For example, an accountant might believe that he lacked sufficient data to estimate the exact net-revenue contributions that a particular good would generate in each year of its estimated service life. Yet he still might believe that these net-revenue contributions would decline sharply with age. If so, he might argue that a declining-charge depreciation pattern was more consistent with what he *was* able to estimate than was straight-line depreciation. Much of the support that has been given to practical employment of declining-charge depreciation rests on this kind of broad application of the net-revenue-contributions approach.[15]

Of course, this kind of broad approach can easily become arbitrary, for reasons discussed in the previous chapter. First, there is the problem of whether the declining-charge method actually chosen is a good approximation to (or surrogate for) the depreciation pattern implicit in whatever the accountant *was* able to estimate. As we have seen, the answer to this question depends at least in part upon decisions about the purpose to be served by the allocations—and these are hard decisions to justify. There is a tendency to employ *any* easily calculated declining-charge method (such as sum-of-the-years'-digits), but ease of calculation alone will not usually be a sufficient defense of an approximation.[16]

---

[13] Most of these are varieties of discounted-contributions valuation. Recently, though, some theorists have begun to recommend an approach identical to the net-revenue-contributions approach except that *current market prices* are allocated, instead of historical acquisition prices. See, for example, AAA (Land), pp. 694–98. This approach is included among the current-price valuation approaches discussed below and in Chapter Six.

[14] Young and Peirson (1967), p. 339.

[15] Here is an example from a textbook:

"Another group of depreciation methods leads to a periodic depreciation charge that declines over an asset's expected life. Methods of this type are appropriate if: (1) the receipts are expected to decline as the asset gets older; and (2) it is believed that the allocation of depreciation should be related to the pattern of the asset's expected receipts."

—Myron J. Gordon and Gordon Shillinglaw, *Accounting, A Management Approach*, Third Edition (Homewood, Illinois: Richard D. Irwin, Inc., 1964), p. 345. See also Wixon and Kell (1960), pp. (17–24); Kohler (1963), pp. 2–3, 179–80; Grady (1965), p. 129; Hendriksen (1965), pp. 325–32; AAA (Land), pp. 696–97; and Reynolds (1961) pp. 245–46.

[16] The reader is reminded of the old anecdote about the gentleman who dropped his watch when returning home at night from the tavern (the light being poor where he dropped his watch, he proceeded to the next street-light before searching for it). Carman made some observations about the accountant's tendency to choose de-

There is also the deeper problem that this kind of situation is one in which the accountant is trying to justify an allocation method in the face of ignorance—partial ignorance, anyway. As we saw in the previous chapter, not only does accounting lack a theory of how to do this, but the circumstances of accounting differ from those of fields in which such theories are presently found.

These problems all spring from a lack of data needed to apply the net-revenue-contributions approach with precision. For reasons given in the next chapter, this study will assume that such data problems do not arise (the main reason for assuming this is that doing so allows us to look at more fundamental questions). Therefore, we may ignore the problems of broad applications of the net-revenue-contributions approach in what follows. But, generally speaking, most of these broad applications would fall into the category of what was described in the previous chapter as attempts at "partial justification," and would not lead to theoretically justified allocation methods.[17]

Nothing in the previous remarks should be taken to imply that the net-revenue-contributions method necessarily is theoretically justified when the requisite data *are* available. By the end of Chapter Five we will have concluded that the net-revenue-contributions approach will usually be arbitrary, regardless of data. For example, in Table 2-2 the investment has an average implicit rate of return of 10 percent per year over its 3-year service life. Chapter Five will demonstrate that this 10 percent average return is consistent with an unlimited number of patterns of individual-year rates of return, each of which averages 10 percent over the three years as a whole. These patterns in turn generate an unlimited number of possible depreciation patterns under the net-revenue-contributions approach . . . and there seems no conclusive way to defend the choice of any one of these patterns against any others. The simplifying assumption whereby the 3-year average rate is chosen as the individual rate within each year is just as arbitrary as, say, the simplifying assumption whereby sum-of-the-years'-digits depreciation is chosen because it is easy to calculate. However, the possibility that the net-revenue-contributions approach is itself arbitrary will be deferred for consideration in later chapters.

3. Other-services approaches

We have been discussing allocations in terms of estimated net-revenue contributions. But perhaps the accountant's immediate concern is with *other* things offered by

---

clining-charge methods for their computational simplicity, above all other properties that an approximation should possess:

". . . they have concocted several bastard schemes, at least two of which are in use. These may be termed segmented schemes for they consist of a series of connected segments of straight lines . . .

" Now segmented schemes have no more *raison d'être* than have square wheels. Their origins are as inglorious as those of a mule."

—Carman (1956), pp. 456, 463. Carman's article has been unduly neglected by subsequent writers, perhaps because of its occasionally hectoring tone. Yet if one wishes to remain within the traditional depreciation framework, his arguments for use of simple polynomial depreciation functions are persuasive. These arguments are not repeated here only because this study concludes that the traditional framework should be abandoned.

[17] Much the same can be said of the use of one of the conventional declining-charge methods to reflect a limited managerial time horizon shorter than the estimated service life of the asset, or to reflect increasing uncertainty in the estimates of net-revenue contributions to be received in successive periods. These possibilities are mentioned in Wixon and Kell (1960), pp. (17–28) – (17–29), and a similar possibility is discussed in an Appendix to Chapter Five. When this kind of justification is given to a declining-charge method, some estimate of the underlying shape of the net-revenue contributions must be made (so that this can be adjusted for increasing uncertainty, for example), *and* the adequacy of the approximation must be defended.

the asset—other services intermediate to any net-revenue contributions.[18] For example, the accountant might be primarily interested in the number of years of service life offered by the machine. Perhaps he has estimated that the machine has a 2-3/4-year service life, and has decided to allocate the machine's $1,100 acquisition price at a rate of $400 per year. Or perhaps he estimates that the machine could be run economically for a total of 11,000 hours, and expects it to be operated 4,000 hours a year for the first two years, and 3,000 hours in Year 3. If so, the particular depreciation pattern chosen ($400-$400-$300) is determined by allocating the machine's acquisition price at a rate of 10¢ an operating hour.

Call these *"other-services approaches"* to depreciation.[19] Two things should be emphasized about other-services approaches:

• 1. These also are ways of allocating historical acquisition prices; they are not valuation approaches.

2. One may interpret these other services either as estimated services that the accountant *expects* will be provided, or as a capacity to provide services, whether or not this capacity is actually used. For example, the accountant might feel that the machine should be depreciated in terms of its 11,000 potential operating hours, even if some of this potential were to be unused and written off to waste.

Much of the accounting literature on depreciation makes no sharp distinction between the net-revenue-contributions approach and the other-services approach. A benefit to future periods is all that is stressed, without inquiring into the *nature* of that benefit.[20] Later in this chapter the two kinds of approach are reconciled.

4. Discounted-contributions valuation approach

The net-revenue-contributions approach uses the historical acquisition price and the estimated net-revenue contributions to determine the implicit rate of return. Once this is done, the historical acquisition price can then be allocated. It is easy to turn this approach into a valuation method. All that is needed is to reduce the net-revenue contributions to a present value by use of some *independently developed* rate of return, then use that present value as the amount to be reported for the good on the balance sheet. Changes in this amount would be reported as depreciation on the income statement. Notice that historical acquisition prices are ignored by this method (except, of course, in making the original purchase decision). The amounts reported are instead the net-revenue-contributions themselves, as discounted to present values. Call this kind of approach *"discounted contributions valuation."*[21]

---

[18] Clear-cut examples of the other-services approach are hard to find. However, see Sprouse and Moonitz (1962), pp. 32–33; Kohler (1963), pp. 144, 169–71, 444–45; Hendriksen (1965), pp. 308–309, 311–12, 319–20; AAA (1957), pp. 539–40; Devine (1962), pp. 260–61; Patrick S. Kemp, "Controversies on the Construction of Financial Statements," *Accounting Review*, XXXVIII (January, 1963), 128–29; and Robert R. Sterling, "Elements of Pure Accounting Theory," *Accounting Review*, XLII (January, 1967), 63–64.

[19] An extreme example of an other-services approach (as well as of the way in which accountants perceive depreciation) was reported in *The Wall Street Journal*, April 15, 1968, p. 17. In a case before the U. S. Tax Court, a Chicago businessman was allowed "to depreciate the airspace in an abandoned clay pit he owned. He was a refuse contractor who was filling the pit with garbage, thereby slowly using up the available dumping space."

[20] For examples, see Wixon and Kell (1960), pp. (16–6)–(16–7), (17–19)–(17–22); Sprouse and Moonitz (1962), pp. 19–21; Grady (1965), pp. 148–50; Hendriksen (1965), pp. 312–13; Peterson (1966), pp. 277–79; and Sybil C. Mobley, "Revenue Experience as a Guide to Asset Valuation," *Accounting Review*, XLII (January, 1967), 114–23.

[21] There is a good description of this approach in Hendriksen (1965), pp. 200–203. In the literature it goes under a number of different names: "valuation by discounted future cash receipts (or service potentials)," "eco-

As an example, suppose that the estimated net-revenue contributions are the same as those given earlier, but that the accountant believes that 6 percent would be an appropriate rate of return for this kind of investment. (This 6 percent could be interpreted either as a target rate that approximates an opportunity rate, or as a cost of capital.) Table 2-3 shows how the value of the machine might be calculated at the end of each year.

TABLE 2-3

VALUATION OF A MACHINE IN TERMS OF ITS ESTIMATED NET-REVENUE CONTRIBUTIONS
10% AVERAGE RATE OF RETURN, 6% DISCOUNT RATE

Time Lapse Before Net-Revenue Contributions Will Occur	6% Discount Factor	Value at Beginning of Year 1		Value at End of Year 1		Value at End of Year 2		Value at End of Year 3	
		Amount	Dis-counted Amount	Amount	Dis-counted Amount	Amount	Dis-counted Amount	Amount	Dis-counted Amount
1 year......	0.9434	$510	$ 481	$470	$443	$330	$311	$-0-	$-0-
2 years......	0.8900	470	418	330	294	-0-	-0-	-0-	-0-
3 years......	0.8396	330	277	-0-	-0-	-0-	-0-	-0-	-0-
			$1,176		$737		$311		$-0-

At the beginning of Year 1, the estimated value of the machine is $76 higher than the amount paid. Unless the purchaser is a "marginal" one, there usually will be this kind of purchaser's surplus.[22] The problems of proper allocation of purchaser's surplus are discussed in Chapter Six—various things could be done with the "extra" $76. Suppose for the present that initially the accountant records the machine at the full $1,176, perhaps recognizing a corresponding $76 gain on purchase. If so, he could then determine the depreciation pattern for this machine simply by letting each year's depreciation charge be the difference between the calculated beginning-of-year and end-of-year values for that year. This is done in Table 2–4.

nomic valuation," "direct valuation," and "time preference analysis." In previous writings I called it the "discounted-services" approach, thereby muddling two different approaches.

Discounted-contributions valuation is often held forth as an ideal by authors who recognize that there are practical barriers to employing it (and who therefore use other methods—most often current-price-valuation methods—as surrogates). For examples of the discounted-contributions approach, both in its pure and in this qualified form, see Hendriksen (1965), pp. 200–203; AAA (Land), p. 694; AAA (Inventory), p. 703; AAA (Basic Theory), p. 34; Gabriel A. D. Preinreich, "Annual Survey of Economic Theory: The Theory of Depreciation," *Econometrica*, VI (July, 1938), 233-39; Diran Bodenhorn, "An Economist Looks at Industrial Accounting and Depreciation," *Accounting Review*, XXXVI (October, 1961), 583–88; Sidney S. Alexander, "Income Measurement in a Dynamic Economy," revised by David Solomons, in Baxter and Davidson (1962), *passim*, especially pp. 148, 175; Donald A. Corbin, "The Revolution in Accounting," *Accounting Review*, XXXVII (October, 1962), 627–33; Stephen A. Zeff, "Replacement Cost: Member of the Family, Welcome Guest, or Intruder?" *Accounting Review*, XXXVII (October, 1962), 620–21; G. Edward Philips, "The Accretion Concept of Income," *Accounting Review*, XXXVIII (January, 1963), 16–17; and Kenneth W. Lemke, "Asset Valuation and Income Theory," *Accounting Review*, XLI (January, 1966), 33–34, 40. Finally, an approach recommended by Wright (and discussed in a later chapter) in effect uses replacement-cost valuation or discounted-contributions valuation, whichever is the lower—see Wright (1964), pp. 82–83.

[22] "The connection between the cost and the capital value of a new machine is by no means a direct one. Its market price oscillates around a balancing point determined marginally by the least efficient pair of all producers and consumers of such machines. In the general case, therefore, capital value is apt to be greater than cost, although fluctuations may temporarily lead to the reverse."
—Preinreich (1938), p. 234, cited by Wright (1967), p. 177 (though without the final clause). See also Devine (1966), pp. 143–44.

TABLE 2-4

DISCOUNTED-CONTRIBUTIONS DEPRECIATION OF A MACHINE

Year	Beginning-of-Year Value	End-of-Year Value	Depreciation Charge
1	$1,176	$737	$ 439
2	737	311	426
3	311	–0–	311
Total			$1,176

5. Current-price valuation approaches

Perhaps, though, the accountant is concerned with the machine's *market* value at the end of each year (instead of the discounted value of its estimated net-revenue contributions). Perhaps the particular depreciation pattern chosen reflects the estimated decline in that market value. There are several senses that could be given to "market value" here: what the company could sell the machine for (exit price), what the company would have to pay to obtain a similar machine (entry price), exit and entry prices of the machine's remaining *services,* and so forth. The various interpretations that have been given the term "replacement cost" would be included among these approaches.

All of these approaches involve market prices *other* than the historical acquisition price of the machine. So, they might be called *"current-price valuation approaches."* This category is something of a catch-all. In Chapter Six we will look at some of the individual depreciation approaches that are to be found within it.[23]

Summary

In summary, present accounting literature includes five main kinds of approaches to depreciation:[24]

    1. arbitrary approaches
    2. net-revenue-contributions approaches
    3. other-services approaches
    4. discounted-contributions valuation approach
    5. current-price valuation approaches

For simplicity, this discussion has ignored several things that complicate the possibilities open to the accountant.

    1. If the accountant believes that a correction for changes in the general price

[23] For examples, see Sprouse and Moonitz (1962), p. 57 and Chapter 4; Hendriksen (1965), pp. 184–87, 203–204, 206–207, 292–97; AAA (Realization), pp. 319–21; AAA (Land), pp. 695–98; AAA (Inventory), pp. 700, 705–706; AAA (Basic Theory), pp. 28–30, 34, 73–95; Bierman (1961), pp. 616–17; Edwards and Bell (1961), pp. 161–88; Wright (1965); A. Goudeket, "An Application of Replacement Value Theory," *Journal of Accountancy,* CX (July, 1960), 38–39; Raymond J. Chambers, *Accounting, Evaluation and Economic Behavior* (Englewood Cliffs, New Jersey: Prentice-Hall, Inc., 1966); L. S. Rosen, "Replacement-Value Accounting," *Accounting Review,* XLII (January, 1967), 106–13; John Leslie Livingstone, "Electric Utility Plant Replacement Costs," *Accounting Review,* XLII (April, 1967), 233–40; and Robert R. Sterling, *The Theory of the Measurement of the Income of Trading Enterprises* (unpublished doctoral dissertation, University of Florida, 1965 [a revised version is forthcoming from the University Press of Kansas]).

[24] These are in addition, of course, to the possibility of ignoring depreciation and charging replacements to current income. This either is an arbitrary approach or is one of the ways to avoid any allocation at all that are discussed in Chapter Six.

level is needed, he may wish to use some kind of common-dollar accounting in calculating depreciation. But this can be done in conjunction with any of these five approaches; common-dollar accounting does not offer a separate depreciation approach in its own right.[25]

2. We have assumed that depreciable assets are not used to manufacture other assets. This restriction may be removed now: the production of an inventory is an "other service" that a depreciable asset may perform. Similarly, we need not assume that the asset has a zero scrap value, for the scrap value is merely an additional service provided by the asset in the year of its retirement.

3. The discussion has been phrased in terms of *ex ante* decisions made by the accountant at the time of purchase. We could instead have phrased it in hindsight, *ex post*, terms had this been desirable—or could instead have regarded the depreciation-pattern decision as one made from year to year, for that matter. The arguments that will be developed later work equally well in all cases, except in Chapter Four, where the point in time of the decision will be important.

Approaches presently used in practice

Present accounting practice uses neither of the two valuation approaches. Present depreciation methods refer to acquisition prices, not values,[26] and these acquisition prices are allocated to income statements by one of the first three methods listed.[27] But present accounting practice is even more limited than this. For the other-services approach cannot be applied independently, but only as one of the first two approaches (arbitrary, or net-revenue contributions).[28] This point is not widely recognized, yet it is fairly easy to demonstrate.

The other-services approach necessitates that the accountant make a series of decisions. First, he must decide *which* other services he will look to. If he wishes to give theoretical justification to his depreciation pattern, presumably he has some theoretical reason for this decision. (The reader will recall the discussion of partial defenses in the previous chapter: to be arbitrary, an approach need not be *opposed* to theory or even wholly indifferent to theory; an arbitrary approach is merely one that lacks a theoretical defense against competing alternatives, so that the choice of

---

[25] The one possible exception to this would be common-dollar systems utilizing very specific indexes. If fixed assets are adjusted by a specific index for the costs of similar fixed assets, common-dollar accounting can become a kind of current-price valuation method. See Eldon S. Hendriksen, "Purchasing Power and Replacement Cost Concepts—Are They Related?" *Accounting Review*, XXXVIII (July, 1963), 483–91, especially 489–90, for the limits within which this is possible. See also Hendriksen (1965), p. 181.

[26] Wixon and Kell (1960), pp. (1–16) − (1–17); Grady (1965), p. 27.

[27] Present accounting practice also may tolerate depreciating the total of the acquisition price plus estimated costs of maintenance—see Wixon and Kell (1960), p. (17–12). This would complicate things, but would not alter the basic description given above. Similarly, there are certain kinds of sinking-fund and annuity-method depreciation approaches that *appear* to depreciate an amount different from the asset's acquisition price. But these all turn out to be versions (though slightly complicated ones) of these three methods. See, for example, Wixon and Kell (1960), pp. (17–25) − (17–27); Kohler (1963), pp. 177–78, 181; and Hendriksen (1965), pp. 322–25.

Lowe points out that sinking-fund and annuity-method approaches *may* be interpreted as depreciation in terms of funds invested, rather than in terms of benefits received—see Lowe (1963), p. 293. Perceived this way, these two approaches no longer fit the framework developed here. But even under this interpretation the problems of ambiguities in rates of return discussed in Chapter Five still apply. And there still is an implicit assumption that a particular pattern of net-revenue contributions can be associated with the asset—an assumption that leads to the same difficulties as those discussed in Chapters Three and Four. Sinking-fund and annuity-method approaches are not discussed in detail in this study because they are no longer widely recommended, but they lead to the same problems as do those methods that *are* actively discussed.

[28] This observation pertains to present practice; naturally; the other-services approach also can be applied in conjunction with the valuation approaches discussed in Chapter Six.

method hinges on some implicit assumption that lacks theoretical justification.)
Suppose that theory leads the accountant to allocate the acquisition price in terms of
the estimated years of service to be provided by the machine. Now the accountant
must make *another* decision: he still must decide how much of the acquisition price
should be associated with each unit of these other services.

If the accountant uses conventional straight-line depreciation, he is associating an
equal amount of acquisition price with each estimated service year. If he uses a conventional declining-charge method, he is associating a varying amount of acquisition
price with each service year. But in either case he has made a decision—he was associated *some* part of the acquisition price with each service year. How does he make
this decision? He *could* make it in an arbitrary way. For instance, he could say that
since he lacks any better answer he will treat all years alike and use straight-line
depreciation. But while this provides a decision, it does so by refusing to answer the
theoretical question. The partially-defended decision is arbitrary—as is any decision
when one refuses to give positive justification for essential choices that are implicit
in what one is doing. If one is going to give theoretical justification to what one does,
it is necessary that *all* parts of one's decision be justified, not just some. (Matters
might be different if the accountant had a systematic theory of appropriate behavior
under ignorance. But, as the previous chapter indicated, such a theory is lacking and,
once again, disciplines which do provide such theories differ from accounting in significant ways.)

Suppose that the accountant wishes to justify the amount that he assigns to each
service year. He can justify his decisions (while continuing to follow conventional
thinking) by either an other-services approach or a net-revenue-contributions approach. If he chooses a second other-services approach, this just pushes the decision
process back another stage, requiring that still *another* decision be made. For example,
suppose that the accountant decides to use conventional straight-line depreciation
because he expects that the machine will be run the same number of hours each year
(or that it will produce the same number of units of product each year, or that it has
the same *capacity* to be run or *capacity* to produce output each year). This decision
still leaves another question unanswered: "Why should each operating hour (or unit
of output or unit of capacity) bear the same share of the acquisition price?"[29] Each

---

[29] Lest the reader think that questions of this kind are empty ones, consider Ponsonby's contention that if an
asset yields units of identical service over its life, those received in early years should have a smaller depreciation
charge associated with them than those received in other years:

"For the value lost in an early year represents the loss of the services which would otherwise have been ren-
dered at the end of its life, that is the present valuation of those possibly 'distant' potential services only. And the
present value of a service to be given at a more distant future time is less than the value of one to be given at a
not so distant future time. This factor would seem to justify putting aside somewhat less per unit of service in the
earlier than in the later years of an asset's life, the actual amount depending on the rate at which future earnings
or benefits are presently discounted."
—Ponsonby (1962), pp. 264–65. (Ponsonby goes on to argue that this effect will usually be more than offset by
increasing costs and inefficiencies of the asset as it ages—a form of the net-revenue-contributions approach.) Of
course, the exact opposite effect would be obtained if one perceived the unit consumed to be the first instead of
the last in the series—compare Hendriksen (1965), pp. 327–28. The problem resembles the FIFO-LIFO problem
with inventories. See also Robert L. Dixon, "Decreasing Charge Depreciation—A Search for Logic," *Accounting
Review*, XXXV (October, 1960), pp. 590–97, for a similar ambiguity.

Goldberg makes the same point as the one made here, but without carrying it through to the same conclusion:

"It should be noted that the idea of allocation of cost has a wider application than . . . one of a periodic charge
of fixed asset cost. Units of activity other than that of a period may be adopted. One might, for example, allocate
the cost of a motor-vehicle over the number of miles travelled or an item of equipment over units of output; and
this could be done over its effective life or over a given period within its effective life. In practice, allocation of

successive question seems as reasonable as the one before. The only way to escape endless regress here (while still following conventional depreciation methods) is to make a *final* decision by either an arbitrary approach or a net-revenue-contributions approach.[30]

A possible objection

The following counter-argument might be raised at this point. Suppose that the accountant is depreciating a single-product machine on a production basis. He might contend that each unit of product benefited equally from the machine. Similarly, each barrel of oil depleted from a reservoir may be the same as every other barrel. It is quite possible that these two propositions could be proven empirically. Would not such proof supply full theoretical justification for use of the production method of depreciation, *without* invoking the net-revenue-contributions approach?[31]

The reply to this is to point out that the argument focuses on the physical benefit provided by the depreciable or depletable asset to the *product*. But the accountant intends to use his depreciation and depletion figures in a report that concerns the net income of the *company*. Therefore, at some stage along the way a relationship must be asserted between benefit-to-the-product and benefit-to-the-company-as-a-whole. Under the justification of the production method given in the previous paragraph, it is implicitly asserted that this relationship is one of simple identity. But clearly this is not necessarily always true: as one of many possible examples, what if the market price of the product has been declining? As was the case in our previous examples, if the production method is to be theoretically justified, one must *defend* one's implicit assumptions.

Similar considerations apply to the various approaches to depreciation suggested by engineers.[32]

Summary

The conclusion that conventional depreciation must either use a net-revenue-contributions approach or be arbitrary may also be defended upon intuitive grounds. Depreciation figures appear on income statements—either directly or as part of cost of goods sold. Though a company may have many goals, its income statement is explicitly designed to reflect only those matters that directly affect income. The

cost is frequently made by superimposing, so to speak, one unit of activity on another, and in this procedure systematic and rational bases are normally used. But however rational the criteria for allocation may be, they are nevertheless arbitrary, in the sense that each allocation represents a selection, determined in accordance with human judgment, out of several possible criteria, some of which may be regarded as having equal validity with the one selected. It is surely desirable to recognize this element of arbitrariness, not because there is anything necessarily objectionable about making arbitrary decisions, but to avoid being misled into thinking that because something appears reasonable it therefore corresponds to objectively verifiable occurrences."
—Goldberg (1962), p. 255. Gellein remarks:

"The constant-charge notion probably appeals to the sense of logic of most people. An asset costing $240 benefits 120 like units; therefore the cost per unit must be $2—that is popular reasoning. This sense of logic, however, may be nothing more than a manifestation of the typical American's sense of equality or maybe his taste for symmetry. It is possible, too, that dislike for a pattern of spreading benefits on some other basis is a result of conflict with long-established tradition."
—Gellein (1955), p. 57. See also Preinreich (1938), p. 219.

[30] One exception to this (a possible appeal to the beliefs of laymen) is discussed in Chapter Six.

[31] Much of Kohler's discussion of cost allocation is in terms similar to these. See Kohler (1963), pp. 144–46, 169–70.

[32] Tangentially to this, see Goldberg's discussion of other problems involved in basing one's allocations in part on what has happened to the asset physically. Goldberg (1962), pp. 253–54.

income statement is not primarily concerned with any of the (non-income) other services provided by assets.[33] We would *expect* it to be difficult to give theoretical justification to any depreciation approach that did not ultimately rest on the effects of the asset on revenues and costs.[34] <u>Conventional depreciation methods must either use a net-revenue-contributions approach or be arbitrary—or else lack theoretical justification of all essential assumptions implicit in the method employed.</u>[35]

The next three chapters will investigate whether the net-revenue-contributions method might not itself be arbitrary, too.

APPENDIX

Net-Revenue Contributions with Multiple Yields

There is an interesting phenomenon which will *not* be discussed in this study, but which resembles something that will receive considerable attention in a later chapter. The particular situation in Table 2-1 is consistent with only one average rate of return. Letting X signify "one plus the interest rate," we can calculate that average rate of return as follows:

$$\$1,100 = \frac{\$510}{X} + \frac{\$470}{X^2} + \frac{\$330}{X^3}$$

$$1,100X^3 = 510X^2 + 470X + 330$$

$$110X^3 - 51X^2 - 47X - 33 = 0$$

$$(X - 1.1)(110X^2 + 70X + 30) = 0$$

---

[33] A similar conclusion was reached by Fess and Ferrara—see Philip E. Fess and William L. Ferrara, "The Period Cost Concept for Income Measurement—Can it Be Defended," *Accounting Review*, XXXVI (October, 1961), 600–601; see also George H. Sorter and Charles T. Horngren, "Asset Recognition and Economic Attributes—The Relevant Costing Approach," *Accounting Review*, XXXVII (July, 1962), 394.

[34] See Delmer P. Hylton, "On Matching Revenue With Expense," *Accounting Review*, XL (October, 1965), 824. Compare Grady (1965) p. 101. The reader is reminded that what we have been calling "net-revenue-contributions" are either net additional revenues or net cost savings—thus their relationship to the income statement.

[35] This conclusion is important to much of the rest of this study. Here is the argument supporting it, restated in a slightly different way. Suppose that an accountant is deciding how to depreciate a newly-acquired machine, *and that he wishes to follow conventional accounting rules*. He *could* make an arbitrary decision—for example, he could decide to depreciate the asset straight-line merely because he depreciates all machines straight-line without worrying about their individual characteristics. Or he could decide to depreciate the machine by the most rapid approach allowed for tax purposes, without worrying whether or not this was really appropriate for income statement purposes. But suppose that the accountant wants to justify his depreciation allocations theoretically (in the sense developed in Chapter One), yet does *not* wish to base his justification on an estimate of the future net revenues or cost savings generated by the machine. The following argument shows that he has wished the impossible. From this impossibility it follows that if the accountant does not want to use an arbitrary approach he *must* use a net-revenue-contributions approach (or else abandon conventional accounting rules).

The reasoning is as follows. The accountant supposedly wishes to defend his depreciation allocations on theoretical grounds, but without basing his defense on the machine's net-revenue contributions. Therefore he must allocate the machine's acquisition price according to some other service or characteristic of the machine—such as its years of service life, the number of units of output that it will produce, or the number of hours that it can be operated.

But, having made *that* decision, the accountant is not yet through. He still must decide how much of the acquisition price should be associated with each service year, each unit of output, or each operating hour. He may decide that some years, units, or hours should have more of the acquisition price associated with them than others. He may decide that all years, units, or hours should bear the same share of the acquisition price. But in either case the accountant is making a decision. In particular, he cannot escape making this decision by treating all years, units, or hours alike, *for doing this is a decision, too*.

How is this decision to be made? If the accountant still does not wish his decision to be arbitrary, he must defend his decision in terms of some *other* characteristic or service of the asset. But this leads to exactly the same

TABLE 2-5

AN INVESTMENT WITH TWO AVERAGE RATES OF RETURN

Year	Estimated Net-Revenue Contributions	Average Rate of Return	Appropriate Discount Factor	Present Value	Average Rate of Return	Appropriate Discount Factor	Present Value
1.....	$2,160	8%	0.9259	$2,000	32%	0.7576	$1,636
2.....	(1,283)	8%	0.8573	(1,100)	32%	0.5739	(736)
				$ 900			$ 900

Since $(110X^2+70X+30)$ lacks real roots, $(X-1.1)$ gives the only average rate of return: $X=1.1$, so the rate of return is $1.1-1.0=10\%$.

But there are patterns of estimated net-revenue contributions that result in *more than one* positive average rate of return on the investment. For example, a company might invest $900 at the beginning of Year 1, expecting thereby to attain cost savings of $2,160 at the end of Year 1, accompanied by *increased* costs of $1,283.04 at the end of Year 2. It turns out that this is consistent with either of *two* average rates of return:

$$\$900 = \frac{\$2,160}{X} - \frac{\$1,283.04}{X^2}$$

$$900X^2 = 2,160X - 1,283.04$$

$$X^2 - 2.4X + 1.4256 = 0$$

$$(X - 1.08)(X - 1.32) = 0$$

The average rates of return are 8% and 32%, as shown in Table 2-5. Similarly, a machine costing $100,000 whose estimated net-revenue contributions are:

Year	Estimated Net-Revenue Contributions
1........................	$ 575,000.00
2........................	(1,321,250.00)
3........................	1,516,562.50
4........................	(869,546.25)
5........................	199,237.50

has average rates of return of 5%, 10%, 15%, 20%, and 25% associated with it.[36]

Algebraically, the existence of multiple yields depends upon some of the estimated net-revenue contributions being positive, others being negative. Therefore, to some extent the existence of multiple yields also depends on the time period chosen for making one's estimates. Consider a profitable but highly seasonal business. If monthly net-revenue contributions were estimated, there might possibly be alternation of

problem as before . . . unless the characteristic or service chosen is the net-revenue contributions associated with the machine. Compare Devine (1962), p. 261.

[36] There are discussions of such multiple yields in John C. Gregory, "Capital Expenditure Evaluation by Direct Discounting," *Accounting Review*, XXXVII (April, 1962), 312–13; and Bierman and Smidt (1966) pp. 44–49. See also C. S. Soper, "The Marginal Efficiency of Capital: A Further Note," *Economic Journal*, LXIX (March, 1959), 174–77, for a discussion where less stringent conditions are set in obtaining a unique rate of return.

negative and positive effects—an alternation which would not occur if *annual* net-revenue contributions were estimated.

Potentially, multiple yields could render the average rate of return ambiguous. However, I doubt that they are an important element in the accountant's allocation problem.[37] This multiple-yield ambiguity should be distinguished from another, much more important, kind of ambiguity in rates of return: the possibility of having only one average rate of return, yet being confronted with a variety of consistent rates of return within individual years. These latter within-year ambiguities are discussed in Chapter Five.

[37] For one reason the ambiguity can be eliminated by explicitly assuming appropriate reinvestment rates—see Victor H. Brown, "Rate of Return: Some Comments on Its Applicability In Capital Budgeting," *Accounting Review*, XXXVI (January, 1961), 54–55. However, this leads to a further ambiguity, which is discussed toward the end of Chapter Four.

CHAPTER THREE

Net-Revenue Contributions: The Simultaneous-Allocation Approach

. . . Why do we allocate cost at all? So far as the accounting procedures are concerned, the currently accepted reply appears to be that the cost of long-term assets is spread as part of the procedure of matching periodic revenues with appropriate charges. Admittedly, this is reasonable and practicable, but it is submitted that it is little more. Can we be sure that it would not be equally reasonable to write off the cost of a long-term asset in the first period after its acquisition—or the last? We say that this should not be done because the asset is used over the period, and, because the asset is so used, the cost should be apportioned according to the use. The services embodied in the physical—or non-physical—asset are yielded up through its use. This is unquestionably reasonable, but it is also based upon assumptions: (a) that the expected benefits will be proportional to an estimated usage rate, and (b) that it is possible to measure the benefits derived from such assets. These assumptions should be brought out into the open for critical inspection.[1]

ONVENTIONAL depreciation must either use a net-revenue-contributions approach or else be arbitrary. But is the net-revenue-contributions approach itself theoretically justified? The next three chapters will demonstrate that this approach almost always leads to serious ambiguities, and that at present these ambiguities cannot be resolved within the framework provided by conventional accounting.[2]

The net-revenue-contributions approach requires estimation of the effect of the particular good on the entity's future revenues or costs. Such estimates are very difficult to make successfully. Yet this study will ignore the estimation problem—*not* because it isn't serious, but because we are going to examine more fundamental difficulties. In fact, for simplicity I will assume throughout what follows that there is *no* significant estimation problem.[3]

---

[1] L. Goldberg, "Concepts of Depreciation," in W. T. Baxter and Sidney Davidson, editors, *Studies in Accounting Theory* (Homewood, Illinois: Richard D. Irwin, Inc., 1962), p. 256.

[2] For general background to this chapter, see R. G. D. Allen, *Mathematical Economics*, Second Edition (London: Macmillan & Co., Ltd., 1965), pp. 332–41, 608–21; and A. A. Walters, "Production and Cost Functions: An Econometric Survey," *Econometrica*, XXXI (January–April, 1963), 1–66. The article by Walters is the classic empirical survey of the literature on production functions. A briefer survey can be found in George H. Hildebrand and Ta-Chung Liu, *Manufacturing Production Functions in the United States, 1957* (Ithaca, New York: New York State School of Industrial and Labor Relations, Cornell University, 1965), pp. 1–3, 19–43.

Solomon Fabricant, "Productivity," in David L. Sills, editor, *International Encyclopedia of the Social Sciences* (New York: The Macmillan Company, 1968), XII, 523–36 is a good introduction both to production functions and to the level of aggregation at which economists discuss them. Devine provides a very sophisticated general discussion of the allocation problem in accounting, one which might be considered in conjunction with any or all of the next four chapters—see Carl Thomas Devine, *Essays in Accounting Theory* (privately printed, 1962), II, 201–16, 241–70. A similar broad background to the discussion in the rest of this book will be found in Richard Mattessich, *Accounting and Analytical Methods* (Homewood, Illinois: Richard D. Irwin, Inc., 1964), pp. 143–61, 184–220.

[3] Strictly speaking, what is assumed is that *ceteris paribus* estimates can be made. It is not assumed that one knows such things as the nature of future technological change.

It should be emphasized that no denial of the estimation problem is made here, nor is there any attempt to

Suppose that a firm owns a collection of depreciable assets, and that its total future revenues and expenses can be estimated with high precision. If we are going to use the net-revenue-contributions approach in depreciating individual assets, we must be able to speak unambiguously of the effect of each asset on net revenues. Now, as the next section will demonstrate, there is more than one sense that could be given to the concept of the net-revenue contributions of an asset.

One very natural sense involves perceiving the accountant as estimating total revenues over the service lives of the depreciable assets, then, for each year, dividing up that year's total revenues, and allocating them to each input factor according to the contribution that each input factor made to the total. Ideally, for any one year it would be possible to obtain figures for the contribution of each input, and the amounts for all inputs would add up to the total revenue for that year.[4] The net-revenue contributions of any *individual* input good over its service life would be the series of annual net-revenue contributions calculated in this way.

Perhaps something like this can be done on a hindsight basis with investments in securities. While valuation of securities poses serious measurement and conceptual problems, it sometimes may be possible to say with little or no ambiguity how much of total securities revenue for any given year results from each individual member of a portfolio (an exception to this is discussed in an appendix to Chapter Five). Unfortunately, it is impossible to allocate total revenues this way for most business firms. Revenues are a joint product of *all* the inputs of a firm, and the attempt at simultaneous allocation of total revenues to all individual inputs leads to much the same difficulties as plague attempts to allocate joint costs.[5]

---

somehow "assume it away" because otherwise it would weaken the conclusions reached. All that is being done is to examine *other* problems without inquiring into the estimation problem. This is legitimate so long as either:

    a) the two problems do not interact; or,
    b) any interactions reinforce our conclusions.

"The basic nature of the periodic income determination problem may best be studied by eliminating the most disturbing factor,—i.e., uncertainty. Once the nature of the process is understood, we may judge any proposed solution to the problems of profit measurement. This is, of course, one of the functions of theory . . . It permits the analysis of basic relationships under the assumption that other factors are held constant."
—Reed K. Storey, "Cash Movements and Periodic Income Determination," *Accounting Review*, XXXV (July, 1960), 449–50. Storey goes on to remark in a footnote (p. 450), "This method is common to all science and is widely used in the analysis of economic problems."

For a good brief discussion of the estimation problem, see Curtis Holt Stanley, *Objectivity in Accounting* (Ann Arbor, Michigan: The University of Michigan, 1965), pp. 50–52. For some additional comments on estimation, see R. J. Chambers, "Measures and Values," *Accounting Review*, XLIII (April, 1968), 240; and Andrew D. Bailey, Jr., and Jack Gray, "A Study of the Importance of the Planning Horizon on Reports Utilizing Discounted Future Cash Flows," *Journal of Accounting Research*, VI (Spring, 1968), 98–105.

[4] The reader should satisfy himself that if allocation is to be made simultaneously to *all* inputs, it is total revenue that must be allocated, not revenue-less-expenses. However, from the standpoint of the individual asset, what is allocated to it *is* the net revenue. For it is net of the contributions made by all other inputs (therefore the designation "net-revenue-contributions" approach).

[5] The AAA Committee on the Matching Concept seems to be saying much the same thing in their discussion of what they call "indirect costs"—see "The Matching Concept," *Accounting Review*, XL (April, 1965), 369–70. There are several other references to this problem in the accounting literature. Diran Bodenhorn, in "An Economist Looks at Industrial Accounting and Depreciation," *Accounting Review*, XXXVI (October, 1961), 586, states the problem neatly; the others (including those works of my own cited below) are at varying levels of rigor. There is a tendency in some works to state the conclusions but ignore their consequences.

See John B. Canning, *The Economics of Accountancy* (New York: The Ronald Press Company, 1929), pp. 232–33; Eugen Schmalenbach, *Dynamic Accounting*, a translation by G. W. Murphy and Kenneth S. Most of *Dynamische Bilanz*, Twelfth Edition (1955), London: Gee and Company Limited, [Publishers] 1959) pp. 26–30; Ronald S. Edwards, "The Nature and Measurement of Income," in Baxter and Davidson (1962), pp. 95–96; Devine (1962) p. 260; Arthur L. Thomas, "Precision and Discounted Services," *Accounting Review*, XXXVII

As we will see in the next section, another possible sense of "the net-revenue contributions of an asset" involves perceiving them as in a capital-budgeting decision, and determining the net-revenue contributions of the asset one asset at a time—as the difference between the series of annual company net incomes (gross of the asset's depreciation) with and without the asset. Unfortunately, as Chapter Four will demonstrate, this approach leads to equally severe problems.

I. The Net-Revenue-Contributions Approach in Detail

Before going any further, we should take a detailed look at the net-revenue-contributions approach and the forms that it might take, so as to see exactly what they involve. To do this, it will be necessary to introduce a few technical concepts.

Production, market, revenue, cost, and income functions[6]

In any firm there is a relationship of some kind between the various economic goods that are the firm's inputs and the economic goods that are its outputs. (The reader will recall that many of these economic goods are services—besides those goods that the accountant would call "assets.") Such a relationship is called a *physical production function*, or just a *production function* for short. Since economic goods (goods that can be bought and sold in a market) are involved, there is a set of *market*

(January, 1962), 67–72; and "Discounted Services Again: The Homogeneity Problem, *Accounting Review*, XXXIX (January, 1964), 1–11 (material from both of these articles has been incorporated in this and the next chapter); F. K. Wright, "Towards a General Theory of Depreciation," *Journal of Accounting Research*, II (Spring, 1964), 87; Felix P. Kollaritsch, "Future Service Potential Value," *Journal of Accountancy*, CXIX (February, 1965), 57–62, and George J. Staubus, letter, *Journal of Accountancy*, CXX (July, 1965), 17–18; J. H. Woods, "Recording Obsolescence: A Note," *Journal of Accounting Research*, III (Autumn, 1965), 262; Carl Thomas Devine, "Asset Cost and Expiration," in Morton Backer, editor, *Modern Accounting Theory* (Englewood Cliffs, New Jersey: Prentice-Hall, Inc., 1966), pp. 142–43, 150; and "Some Conceptual Problems in Accounting Measurements," in Robert K. Jaedicke, Yuji Ijiri, and Oswald Nielsen, editors, *Research in Accounting Measurement* (Evanston, Illinois: American Accounting Association, 1966), pp. 25–26; Kenneth W. Lemke, "Asset Valuation and Income Theory," *Accounting Review*, XLI (January, 1966), 34; T. N. Young and C. G. Pierson, "Depreciation—Future Services Basis," *Accounting Review*, XLII (April, 1967), 338; and Orace Johnson, "Two General Concepts of Depreciation," *Journal of Accounting Research* (Spring, 1968), p. 36.

Recently, Carsberg has discovered an article in *The Accountant* for 1913 in which a similar observation may have been made; see Bryan V. Carsberg, "The Contribution of P. D. Leake to the Theory of Goodwill Valuation," *Journal of Accounting Research*, IV (Spring, 1966), 8. (See also pp. 11–12 for Carsberg's own views.) But did this 1913 author really see the allocation issue clearly? Here is the closest that he comes. A business has been purchased for $25,000, of which $5,000 is allocated to goodwill:

". . . you consider the business worth $25,000, and that on the basis of earnings; the all-important point in your mind is earning power. If this be true, upon what rational basis can you say that $20,000 resides definitely in plant, equipment, merchandise, &c. while $5,000 is an ethereal, shadowy something, goodwill? Do you not pay the $25,000 for the business as it appears, for the returns which you are reasonably certain to get? Do you not consider it the present value that you place upon the future income of the business? Why, fundamentally, should it be considered part tangible and part intangible?" [From an American Correspondent], "Goodwill: its Nature, Value, and Treatment in the Accounts," *The Accountant*, XLIX (December 6, 1913), 817. Is Carsberg correct when he says (p. 8) that this author:

". . . pointed out that usually the value of a business lay primarily in its anticipated future earnings, and claimed that it was impossible to demonstrate a uniquely correct apportionment of that value between individual assets."?

Or is the 1913 author less precise than this?

The parallel to problems of joint-cost allocation may be made more exact by observing that joint products may either be prepared in fixed proportions (as with left and right shoes from a single piece of leather), or variable proportions (as with many products of petroleum refineries). The allocation of revenues to joint inputs is similar to the *variable proportions* kind of joint-cost allocation problem.

[6] The concepts discussed in this subsection are related to standard concepts from economic theory. A good concise discussion of production and market functions can be found in Kenneth E. Boulding, *A Reconstruction of Economics* (New York: Science Editions, Inc., 1962 [paperback reprint of original edition, New York: John Wiley & Sons, Inc., 1950]), p. 34, upon which the following is partly modeled. See also Fabricant (1968).

functions which relate the quantities of inputs and outputs to their prices. A firm's production and market functions may change over time—in fact ordinarily we would expect them to do so.

By combining the market functions for the firm's outputs with its production function, one obtains a *revenue function* reflecting the relationship between the firm's gross revenues and the economic goods inputs that generate these revenues. As we saw in Chapter One, under conventional accounting rules the costs that are matched with a firm's revenues are not determined directly from the current market functions for the firm's inputs. Instead, the *cost function* is developed by combining the market function for each input at the time of its acquisition by the firm with an *allocation rule*. (The reader will recall that this description is true even of those economic goods whose acquisition prices the accountant allocates to a single year.)

Finally, under conventional accounting rules, the firm's *net income function*, or *income function* for short, results from combining the firm's revenue function with its cost function.[7] Of course, the various functions discussed here may be very complicated, and there may be great practical difficulties in estimating them. But *some* such set of relationships lies beneath the figures that appear on any income statement.

The net-revenue-contributions approach

In the net-revenue-contributions approach, the acquisition price of the asset is known. The problem is to allocate that acquisition price to the years that make up the asset's service life. (For simplicity, it will be assumed again that there is no scrap value upon the asset's retirement.) The method requires knowledge of the estimated net-revenue contributions of the asset in each year of its service life. These, in conjunction with the acquisition price, are used to determine the (average) implicit rate of return on the investment in the asset.

The amount at which the asset is reported on the annual balance sheet is its *book value*. Under the net-revenue-contributions approach, this book value will at all times be the sum of the asset's estimated net-revenue contributions not yet received, discounted to a present value at the implicit rate of return. Depreciation for any year will equal the difference between the asset's beginning and ending book values. As this chapter and the next will demonstrate, there are two ways in which the estimated net-revenue contributions might be calculated:

1. For each year, the firm's revenues, gross of all expenses, might be allocated to all individual inputs simultaneously. To do this, one must estimate the revenue function for each year of the assets' service lives. Also, as we will see later in this chapter, the nature of the revenue function must be such that allocation of total revenue to all individual inputs will not be arbitrary. This process must be applied to each year. We will call it the *simultaneous-allocation* approach.

2. Alternately, at the time when the asset is purchased one could estimate the pattern of the firm's *net incomes* during the asset's service life, assuming that the asset had not been acquired, then estimate a corresponding sequence of net incomes (gross of the depreciation of the asset) given the acquisition and use of the asset. In each year the asset's net-revenue contribution would be the difference between the net income from the second sequence and the net income from the first. We will call this the *capital-budgeting* approach to calculating the net-revenue contributions, since

---

[7] For simplicity, certain kinds of non-operating gains and losses are ignored in this discussion.

firms may calculate them this way in the process of deciding whether to purchase the asset.

Notice that under either approach there are *two* different allocations involved in the net-revenue contributions approach. First, revenue or net income is allocated to inputs. In the capital-budgeting approach the entire allocation is to the *one* asset but (as will be stressed in the next chapter) a 100 percent allocation is as much an allocation as any other. Then these allocations and the acquisition price are used to calculate the implicit rate of return. Having done this, a *second* allocation is performed, whereby the acquisition price is divided among the estimated years of service. Call these two allocations respectively the *contributions allocation* and the *depreciation allocation*. Under the net-revenue-contributions approach, two ways are proposed for making the contributions allocation (simultaneous-allocation and capital-budgeting) and one way to make the depreciation allocation. This chapter discusses the simultaneous-allocation approach; Chapter Four discusses the capital-budgeting approach; Chapter Five discusses the depreciation allocation.

The algebra of the net-revenue-contributions approach

To avoid possible ambiguity, the material discussed in the previous subsection is presented algebraically below. The algebra is elementary, but some of its notation is used later in this study. (Scrap values are ignored.)

K_j = the acquisition price of any depreciable asset, j, acquired at the beginning of Year 1

N = the estimated service life of asset j, in years

$B_j(t)$ = the book value of asset j at the end of Year t

$Y(t)$ = the firm's total revenue in Year t

$Y_j(t)$ = the estimated net-revenue contribution of asset j in Year t

$r_j(t)$ = the implicit rate of return on the investment in asset j in Year t (really, the *average* rate of return during this year)

$D_j(t)$ = the depreciation charge for asset j in Year t

$X_i(t)$ = the number of units of input i used in Year t

$f(t)$ = the firm's revenue function in Year t

$Z^0(t)$ = the amount of the firm's net income in Year t, assuming that asset j had not been acquired

$Z'(t)$ = the amount of the firm's net income (gross of the depreciation of asset j) in Year t, assuming that asset j had been acquired and used.

In conventional accounting, depreciation is a process of allocating K_j over the N periods, such that:

$$K_j = \sum_{t=1}^{N} D_j(t)$$

Chapter Two showed that for a conventional depreciation method to be theoretically justified, it must allocate K_j in terms of asset j's estimated net-revenue contributions. The method for doing this proposed by theorists is as follows. First, it is assumed that:

$$r_j(1) = r_j(2) = \cdots = r_j(N) = r_j,$$

the *average* implicit rate of return on the investment in asset j (really, the average rate of return during the entire service life of asset j). Then r_j is computed as that number such that:

$$K_j = \sum_{t=1}^{N} \frac{Y_j(t)}{(1 + r_j)^t}$$

The book value of the asset at the end of Year h is, therefore:

For $h = 0$: $B_j(0) = K_j$

For $h = 1, 2, \cdots, N$: $B_j(h) = \sum_{t=h+1}^{N} \frac{Y_j(t)}{(1 + r_j)^{t-h}}$

There are two ways in which the $Y_j(t)$ might be determined:

1. *Simultaneous allocation.* The firm's total revenues for the year might be allocated to all individual inputs $i = 1, 2, \cdots, j, \cdots, m$ simultaneously. To do this, it is necessary to know the revenue function for each Year t:

$$Y(t) = f(t)[X_1(t), \cdots, X_j(t), \cdots, X_m(t)]$$

and it must be possible to allocate $Y(t)$ to each of the $X_i(t)$ simultaneously without arbitrariness. This process must be applied to each year.

2. *Capital-budgeting allocation.* Alternately, at the time asset j is purchased one could estimate the firm's future *net income* sequence, $Z^0(t)$, $t = 1, \cdots, N$, assuming that asset j had not been acquired. Then a corresponding sequence $Z'(t)$, $t = 1, \cdots, N$, representing the net income sequence (gross of the depreciation of asset j) given the acquisition and use of asset j could be estimated. Having made these estimates:

$$Y_j(t) = Z'(t) - Z^0(t)$$

In either event, the depreciation charge for asset j in Year t will be:

$$D_j(t) = B_j(t - 1) - B_j(t)$$

II. The Interaction Problem

The rest of this chapter examines the circumstances under which the contributions allocation can be justified using a simultaneous-allocation approach. Here is the problem, restated in non-algebraic language. A firm's future revenues for a number of years have been estimated. In each year the firm will employ a number of inputs, among which is included the depreciable asset. How is the total revenue to be allocated to the individual inputs?

An appeal to the layman will not help here. There are no rules upon which intelligent laymen would agree except, possibly, that each input should have allocated to it those revenues that it causes—and this just restates the problem without answering it. When we appeal to economic theory, three approaches are presently available:

1. simple additive allocation,
2. allocation based upon linear programming and activity analysis,
3. allocation based upon the marginal approach.

It is possible that other approaches will be developed in the future; but these are the only ones available *now*.

1. *Simple additive allocation*

To see what simple additive allocation involves, suppose that a company manufactures a single product, using two inputs, X_1 and X_2, and that the revenue function is the following (unrealistic) one in all years:[8]

$$Y = 3X_1 + 11X_2 \qquad (X_1, X_2 \leq 10)$$

Suppose that the firm maximizes revenue (at $140) by using 10 of each kind of input. The net-revenue contributions of the two different kinds of inputs are obvious: $30 from the X_1's and $110 from the X_2's; the allocation is unambiguous and defensible, and it divides up the entire $140 revenue.

Interaction

But suppose that, instead, the revenue function were:

$$Y = 3X_1 + X_1X_2 + X_2 \qquad (X_1, X_2 \leq 10)$$

and that the firm again maximizes revenues (at $140) by using 10 of each kind of input. One still can say that $30 of the revenue is the separate effect of the X_1's, and that $10 is the separate effect of the X_2's. But $100 is an *interaction* effect of the X_1's and X_2's combined, and there is no simple defensible way to allocate this $100 to the individual inputs.[9] This leads to a dilemma. We *can* speak of separate net-revenue-contributions of the individual inputs, but only in a way that violates a requirement for allocations. The *entire* $140 results from the X_1's and X_2's employed, not just $40; it is arbitrary to base one's allocations of the acquisition prices of these inputs on a contributions allocation that ignores most of the revenue *contributed* by these inputs. If we wish somehow to divide up the "extra" $100, there are various ways to do so, each of which seemingly would be as plausible as any other.[10]

Of course, one could artificially perceive the X_1X_2 interaction as a third kind of input. We will examine this possibility later. But it should immediately be obvious that doing so would require a substantial departure from present accounting rules. At present, accountants report on inputs individually; were they also to report interactions, their reports would become vastly more complicated.[11]

Interaction effects are widespread in most firms at the level of input aggregation faced by the accountant.[12] Any statistician doing variance analysis is familiar with

---

[8] Throughout the discussion in this and the next chapter, highly simplified illustrations will be used to avoid swamping the exposition in a lot of unnecessary mathematics. However, over their totality the examples have been chosen to incorporate those features of more realistic models that affect the issues under consideration. Part of the problem in preparing illustrations (as emphasized later in this chapter) is that economic theory does not *provide* suitable models at the level of aggregation faced by the accountant.

[9] It is argued later in this chapter that there presently is no defensible way *whatever* to perform this allocation, but this argument need not be anticipated at this point.

[10] Consider, for example, the problems of defending a 1:1 allocation against someone who preferred a 3:1 allocation, or vice versa. An appeal to economic theory here will be examined when we discuss the marginal approach.

[11] Simple combinatorial mathematics show that if the accountant recognizes 30 different kinds of inputs (a conservative figure) there will be 435 possible two-input interactions, 4,060 possible three-input interactions, 27,405 possible four-input interactions, and so forth.

[12] See, for example, Canning (1929), pp. 232–33; Zenon S. Zannetos, "Mathematics as a Tool of Accounting Instruction and Research," *Accounting Review*, XXXVIII (April, 1963), 333–35; Tjalling C. Koopmans, *Three Essays on the State of Economic Science* (New York: McGraw-Hill Book Company, Inc., 1957), p. 75. For related problems of empirical estimation because of multicollinearity of factors, see Robert E. Jensen, "A Multiple Regression Model for Cost Control—Assumptions and Limitations," *Accounting Review*, XLII (April, 1967), 271.

this (so is any manager, say, whose decision to buy machinery has been influenced by his labor situation). Any time a new asset is purchased, the productivity of previously owned assets is apt to change. So does the productivity of other inputs not reported as assets—labor, for example. The assumption that interaction effects are *not* present implies that the input's contribution to revenues would be the same even if it were divorced from the firm.[13] There are a few inputs (such as incidental investments in securities) of which this may be true. But ordinarily the assumption of independence is patently false.

This, of course, is an additional reason why a contributions allocation that looks only to the separate effects of the inputs is improper. Such an allocation leads to depreciating the asset in terms of a pattern of net-revenue contributions that are the residuals of treating the asset as though it were independent of all other inputs. Actually, of course, it is not. Should we choose to *define* the net-revenue contribution of an asset as its residual independent effects, then we would still have to justify the choice of this *portion* of the total revenue instead of its totality (and the reply that allocation of the totality is impossible will really not do as justification—since, as emphasized before, the point at issue is whether *any* allocations can be theoretically justified). I can think of no way to defend this choice that does not lead to endless regress. (A final example of the arbitrariness of a contributions allocation that looks only to the separate effects of the inputs is given in Note 33 to this chapter: There are many plausible revenue functions in which the separate effects of some or all essential inputs will be *negative*, even though total revenue is positive!)

Therefore, the conclusion is that simple additive allocation will provide theoretical justification for the contributions allocation only in those rare cases where input interactions do not occur or are unimportant enough to be ignored. Typically, this is not a way in which the net-revenue-contributions approach can be justified.

2. Linear programming and activity analysis

The same problem of interactions plagues any attempt to justify the contributions allocation by linear activity analysis. Koopmans has an interesting discussion of the basic postulates of linear activity analysis.[14] Linear activity analysis is, first of all, *linear*. It perceives the production function as a set of basic processes that never interact with each other, which are additive and independent. The following postulates are from Koopmans' work cited immediately above:

1. Each input and output must be " . . . *homogeneous* in the sense that equal amounts are interchangeable in all their uses." (p. 73)

2. Additivity is assumed. "The implication of this postulate is one of noninteraction between productive processes. Given the resources required for each of two methods of production, both can be engaged in simultaneously without either one of them affecting the outcome of the other." (pp. 74–75) Koopmans goes on to emphasize the likelihood of interaction between processes, suggesting " . . . lumping together the interacting activities into one single activity . . ." (p. 75) as a possible expedient (one which we will examine later).

3. As indicated immediately above, proportionality is assumed. But " . . . this postulate implies . . . that the null activity (with no inputs or outputs) is possible.

---

[13] See Mordecai Ezekiel and Karl A. Fox, *Methods of Correlation and Regression Analysis* (New York: John Wiley & Sons, Inc., 1959), pp. 348–52, for good background to this point.

[14] See Koopmans (1957), pp. 72–77, as well as Walters (1963), pp. 2–4; and Allen (1965), pp. 332–37, 618–21.

Generally, the postulate implies what is known as constant returns to the scale of production." (p. 76)

The phenomenon of fixed inputs faced by the accountant makes the null activity assumption open to question. Constant returns to scale may be required for *equilibrium*. But it is not at all clear that they are what the accountant faces in dealing with the actual firm.[15]

In general, there are strong reasons to believe that the situations faced by the financial accountant violate the basic postulates of linear activity analysis, in particular the additivity postulate (see the discussion of interactions effects in the previous subsection). This is concluded despite the fact that several writers with whom one hesitates to disagree have seen promise in this approach (and in related uses of matrix algebra for cost allocations—especially for overhead cost allocations).[16]

Once again, linear activity analysis can be used in performing the contributions allocation *if* matters like interaction effects are ignored. But interaction effects are important and pervasive—as the mental experiment of divorcing most inputs from the firm will demonstrate. Much of the contribution to net revenues provided by an input is an interaction effect. A depreciation method that supposedly is justified by the net-revenue-contributions approach, and which ignores a major portion of these contributions, clearly must justify the omission. If much of the contributions are joint and *cannot* be recognized by the method, the obvious conclusion is that the method will not work. There is no apparent reason to conclude instead that depreciation should be calculated in terms of the residual portion that *can* be recognized.

---

[15] Even in the highly aggregated industry cases examined by Hildebrand and Liu, the bulk of the industries examined were experiencing increasing returns to scale. See Hildebrand and Liu (1965), pp. 6–7, 106–10.

[16] See Nicholas Dopuch, "Mathematical Programming and Accounting Approaches to Incremental Cost Analysis," *Accounting Review*, XXXVIII (October, 1963), 745–53; Nicholas Dopuch, Jacob G. Birnberg, and Joel Demski, "An Extension of Standard Cost Variance Analysis," *Accounting Review*, XLII (July, 1967), 526–36; Joel S. Demski, "An Accounting System Structured on a Linear Programming Model," *Accounting Review*, XLII (October, 1967), 701–12. The reader also should see Mattessich (1964) pp. 197–98, for a discussion of those areas in which accounting applications *may* exist.

A distinction should be made at this point. The foregoing comments pertain to linear activity analysis as an independent theoretical approach to allocation. Of course linear algebra may be used (as may any appropriate mathematical tool) in carrying out *other* allocation methods. For example, if the cost accountant already has somehow established a set of reciprocal relationships among producing and service departments, it may be possible to distribute service department costs by use of matrix algebra, rather than by the traditional method of successive iteration. This is possible *whatever* were the methods used in establishing the basic set of reciprocal relationships (typically, the ordinary techniques of the cost accountant are assumed to have been used). Here, linear algebra is just a computational tool. For three good examples of this approach, see Thomas H. Williams and Charles H. Griffin, "Matrix Theory and Cost Allocation," *Accounting Review*, XXXIX (July, 1964), 671–78; Neil Churchill, "Linear Algebra and Cost Allocations: Some Examples," *Accounting Review*, XXXIX (October, 1964), 894–904; and Rene P. Manes, "Comment on Matrix Theory and Cost Allocation," *Accounting Review*, XL (July 1965), 640–43.

Besides the remarks already made, the following observation by Zannetos is pertinent:

"All of us are aware that the methods used for fixed overhead allocations are arbitrary. In using matrix algebra, the percentages of the costs that we feel should go to the various activities are used as inputs in the matrix that will be inverted for solving the simultaneous equations. Now do we really gain anything by such "exactness"? Definitely not! While there is no doubt that we preserve mathematical integrity in the application (programming) of imperfect decision rules, we must not lose sight of the value of the information that we so obtain." —Zannetos (1963), p. 333; see also Douglas Vickers, "On the Economics of Break-Even," *Accounting Review*, XXXV (July, 1960), 410–12, for a discussion of non-linearity and *irreversibility* in cost and revenue functions.

3. The marginal approach

There is one allocation method (suggested by economic theory) that can incorporate interaction effects. However, it can do so only under certain rigid conditions. And an argument can be developed that even when these conditions are met, the resulting allocations are arbitrary.

The contributions allocation might be performed in terms of the *marginal* contributions made by the inputs.[17] These marginal contributions can be calculated by taking the partial derivatives of the revenue function with respect to each input, and solving by substituting the actual amounts of each kind of input employed. Using the notation developed earlier (in which $X_i(t)$ is the number of units of input i used in Year t), if the revenue function in Year t is:

$$Y(t) = f(t)[X_1(t), \cdots, X_j(t), \cdots, X_m(t)]$$

then the marginal contribution of the last unit of input i is $M_i(t)$, such that:

$$M_i(t) = \frac{\partial Y(t)}{\partial X_i(t)}$$

evaluated at the actual levels of $X_1, \cdots, X_j, \cdots, X_m$ in Year t. The portion of $Y(t)$ to be allocated to input i is:

$$M_i(t) \cdot X_i(t)$$

In particular:

$$Y_j(t) = M_j(t) \cdot X_j(t)$$

The above process must be applied to each year, $t = 1, \cdots, N$.

Restrictions on this approach

Just as linear activity analysis has certain implicit assumptions, so the marginal contributions approach requires that the revenue function satisfy certain conditions. The marginal approach requires continuously differentiable functions and cannot handle inequality constraints. It assumes infinitely varying input proportions—i.e., continuous rate of substitution. Also, it requires that the revenue function possess a mathematical property called linear homogeneity. The discussion of this property, and why it is required under the marginal contributions approach, will be found in the Appendix to this chapter. Linear homogeneity may be equated with the economists' concept of constant returns to scale. (The notion has little to do with "homogeneity" in the ordinary sense of "thoroughly mixed" or "fungible.")

---

[17] "The relevant future net receipts would be the *marginal* net receipts associable with the asset in question—not the total net receipts attributable to the single asset as though it were bereaved of the firm."
—Stephen A. Zeff, "Replacement Cost: Member of the Family, Welcome Guest, Or Intruder?" *Accounting Review*, XXXVII (October, 1962), 624n; see also Stephen A. Zeff and W. David Maxwell, "Holding Gains on Fixed Assets—A Demurrer," *Accounting Review*, XL (January, 1965), 67; and Bodenhorn (1961), p. 586 (the reader should note that Bodenhorn is discussing things at a different level of aggregation than we are here). In presenting earlier versions of this study before various audiences, I have found a widespread belief that marginal contributions are appropriate to the problem; the arguments offered parallel those for using marginal costs in allocating joint costs, when joint products are made in variable proportions. For an example, see John S. Chiu and Don T. DeCoster, "Multiple Product Costing by Multiple Correlation Analysis," *Accounting Review*, XLI (October, 1966), 674–75.

If the revenue function is *non*homogeneous (or homogeneous, but not linear homogenous), and the marginal contributions approach is employed in the contributions allocation, an implicit assumption of the marginal contributions approach is violated. Attempts to allocate revenues to individual inputs continue to be *mechanically* feasible, as far as the calculations go. But the results are arbitrary.[18] A variety of conflicting alternative methods will be available for allocating the revenue, with no conclusive way to defend any one against all the others.

A nonhomogeneous example will illustrate this point. Suppose that there are just two kinds of inputs, P's and Q's, and that the revenue function for Year t is the following nonhomogeneous one:

$$Y(t) = f(P, Q) = 20\,P - P^2 + 3PQ + 13Q - 6Q^2$$

where $Y(t)$ is the total revenue in Year t, and P and Q are the numbers of units of the respective inputs used in Year t. Suppose that the firm uses ten P's and four Q's. Total revenue is $(200-100+120+52-96) = \$176$. Using the marginal approach (as discussed in the Appendix to this chapter) it turns out that the marginal contribution of each unit of P is \$12, while that of each unit of Q is a *negative* \$5, for a total marginal contribution of \$100, as compared with the total revenues of \$176.[19]

Why is marginal contributions allocation arbitrary in such cases? Not because one *can't* allocate in some way or another, but because (as is traditionally claimed of allocations of joint costs) there is an embarrassment of riches—too many equally defensible (or indefensible) possibilities. The total marginal contributions differ from the total revenue; there are a number of incompatible ways to handle this discrepancy, but no conclusive way to defend the choice of any one method over all the others. One might allocate \$1.76 of revenue for each dollar of marginal contributions (though this would result in negative net-revenue contributions and a kind of liabilities treatment for the Q inputs). Or one might allocate the "extra" \$76, 10/14ths to the P's and 4/14ths to the Q's. Or one might allocate in terms of *absolute* marginal contributions, at a rate of 176/140 dollars of revenue for each absolute dollar of marginal contributions. Or one might follow any one of a number of other possible

---

[18] The difficulty here resembles one often encountered in statistics. Statistical methods embody implicit assumptions about the nature of the phenomena being examined. If the actual data violate these assumptions, one still can go ahead and perform the calculations. But the results often will be nonsense. A good description of this problem can be found in Jensen (1967) pp. 269–73.

[19] This is true even though the Q's add \$76 to total revenue! Total revenue from 10 P's and *no* Q's would be only $(200-100+0+0+0) = \$100$. The calculations behind this example are:

$$\frac{\partial f(P, Q)}{\partial P} = 20 - 2P + 3Q \qquad \frac{\partial f(P, Q)}{\partial Q} = 3P + 13 - 12Q$$

Substituting $P=10$, $Q=4$, we get:

Kind of Input	Marginal Contribution	Number of Units Used	Total
P..........	\$12	10	\$120
Q..........	(5)	4	(20)
Total...			\$100
Revenue...			\$176

allocation systems. Neither economic theory nor the kinds of rules upon which lay-men would agree provide any conclusive way to defend one's choice here, so any method chosen will be arbitrary.[20] As the appendix to this chapter demonstrates, one gets into much the same difficulties unless the revenue function is *linear* homogeneous. i.e., characterized by constant returns to scale. In general, unless the revenue function is linear homogeneous, use of the marginal contributions approach to the contributions allocation will lead to arbitrary results.

Are accounting's revenue functions linear homogeneous?

Therefore, it becomes important to ask whether the kinds of revenue functions that confront accountants are apt to be linear homogeneous. The issue of homogeneity will be considered first, before worrying about *linear* homogeneity.

An appeal to economic theory provides surprisingly little help in deciding whether revenue functions are homogeneous. In economic theory the firm is discussed at a very different level of aggregation than it is in financial accounting. There is little or no concern over what might be called the "fine structure" of the firm—its individual inputs. Boulding comments:

... as generally presented in the textbooks the firm is a strange bloodless crea-ture without a balance sheet, without any visible capital structure, without debts, and en-gaged apparently in the simultaneous purchase of inputs and sale of outputs at constant rates.[21]

Explicit recognition is given to very few different kinds of inputs. The previously mentioned study by Hildebrand and Liu uses more variables than most, yet its industry production functions employ only the following:

> Capital
> Production labor
> Nonproduction labor
> A proxy variable for technological change
> A random disturbance term.[22]

In fact, usually there isn't any necessity that the economists' discussion even refer to an individual firm at all—the functions could just as well be those of an industry, or even of a whole national economy. A study of Walters' survey of production func-

---

[20] As a somewhat similar situation, consider the student who gets a *C*, two *D*'s, and two *F*'s, and who flunks out of school. We all know that, no matter what he says, no *one* course caused his suspension—it was a joint result of what happened in all of his courses. Any attempt to pin the responsibility on any individual course is essentially meaningless. Similarly, when the revenue function is nonhomogeneous, it is essentially meaningless to speak of allocating revenue to individual inputs.

Billy Goetz provides some valuable examples of how, in a different situation than those discussed here, one gets into serious problems if one tries to make allocations when the relationships are nonhomogeneous. See Billy E. Goetz, "Transfer Prices: An Exercise in Relevancy and Goal Congruence," *Accounting Review*, XLII (July, 1967), 435–40.

[21] Boulding (1962), p. 34. Preinreich made a similar comment directed specifically to depreciation:

"Mathematical economists have excogitated more or less fine-spun applications of the law of capital value to so-called capital assets, but most of their attention appears to have been devoted to the economic behavior of a single "machine," rather than to the continuous flow of productive assets through a plant or production center. There has been great interest in why the economic life or usefulness of a machine reaches its end, but compara-tively little in the mass phenomena of how gradual consumption actually occurs."

—Gabriel A. D. Preinreich, "Annual Survey of Economic Theory: The Theory of Depreciation," *Econometrica*, VI (July, 1938), 219.

[22] See Hildebrand and Liu (1965), Chapter III.

tions[23] should convince the reader that most economists' production functions involve a degree of aggregation that makes them unsuitable for use in the accountant's reports. As Cohen observes:

Economic models which are designed to answer one class of question may be inadequate or inappropriate for answering questions involving a different level of aggregation. The neoclassical theory of the firm has been designed primarily to answer questions concerning ways in which resources are allocated among industries within a free price economy. While the neoclassical model may be quite adequate for this purpose, there are, of course, large categories of interesting economic questions which cannot satisfactorily be answered by this model.[24]

As far as homogeneity goes, instead of investigating whether it is present or not, economists are far more apt simply to *assume* that it exists, in order to be able to make their calculations. The following comment by Solow is a straight-forward example:

Since we have assumed that factors are paid their marginal products, this amounts to assuming the hypotheses of Euler's theorem. The calculus being what it is, we might just as well assume the conclusion, namely that F is homogeneous of degree one. This has the advantage of making everything come out neatly in terms of intensive magnitudes.[25]

Polynomial revenue functions

Lacking much help from economic theory, the discussion of the homogeneity of accounting's revenue functions must necessarily be a bit sketchy. But a few things are clear. As the Appendix to this chapter points out, for a *polynomial* revenue function to be homogeneous, its terms must all be of the same degree. (As examples, a constant is of degree zero, X is of degree one, X^2 and XY are both of degree two, and so forth.) If revenue is simultaneously to be allocated to *all* inputs (as the simultaneous-allocation approach requires), then the revenue function must explicitly include all inputs. Some of these inputs will be fixed, some will be variable.[26] The

---

[23] Walters (1963).

[24] Kalman J. Cohen, "Simulation of the Firm," *American Economic Review*, L (May, 1960), 535.

[25] Robert M. Solow, "Technical Change and the Aggregate Production Function," *Review of Economics and Statistics*, XXXIX (August, 1957), 313.

[26] The words "fixed" and "variable" are being used in the following sense. Within any one-year period, an input is "fixed" if it does not vary with a change in output, "variable" if it varies proportionately to a change in output. These are not necessarily the same as the related distinctions traditionally made by accountants. In accounting, whether or not an input is fixed often depends upon the particular accounting method employed; for example, machine depreciation will be variable if production depreciation is being used, and fixed otherwise. Stenason and Bandeen's study of Canadian railway costs gives some good examples of the kind of fixed-variable distinction that is being made here. By use of regression analysis (and a few other techniques) the authors found that yard-crew and train-crew wages were completely variable with traffic volume; so was fuel expense for road and yard diesel locomotives. On the other hand, costs like those of maintenance of fences, snow sheds and signs, and costs of snow, sand, and ice removal were found not to vary with traffic volume. See W. J. Stenason and R. A. Bandeen, "Transportation Costs and Their Implications: An Empirical Survey of Railway Costs in Canada," in *Transporatation Economics* (New York: National Bureau of Economic Research, 1965), pp. 121–38. There is a shorter, but similar, discussion in John R. Meyer, Merton J. Peck, John Stenason, and Charles Zwick, *The Economics of Competition in the Transportation Industries* (Cambridge, Massachusetts: Harvard University Press, 1959), pp. 23–24. Douglas Vickers quotes a categorization of costs suggested by K. J. Arkwright that summarizes the variety of fixed costs incurred by the typical manufacturing firm:

"He suggests the following sixfold categories: (a) unitary variable costs, which increase by one cost unit with each increase of one production unit; (b) non-unitary variable costs, which change by more or less than one cost unit with each unit change of production; (c) cost of reserve capacity necessarily incurred to cater for short-term fluctuations in the level of activity; (d) irregular independent costs which are completely irregular in amount and

related terms in the revenue function will, therefore, be of different degree.[27] The necessity to incorporate interaction terms in the revenue function makes it even more unlikely that all polynomial terms will be of the same degree—the reader is invited to verify this for himself. In summary, for a polynomial revenue function explicitly to include those features of the firm with which financial accountants must deal, the function must usually be nonhomogeneous.

Cobb-Douglas functions

The reader is reminded that a revenue function results from combining a production function with market functions for the firm's outputs. Consider the production function. In one form or another, the Cobb-Douglas function is the most popular production function in the economics literature:[28]

$$Z = aL^\alpha K^\beta$$

where Z represents output, L the quantity of labor, K the quantity of capital, α and β are exponents, and a is a constant. This function is homogeneous. But once again the representation of fixed factors becomes a problem. If we include them in the *form* of the production function[29] it is hard to see how (in the related revenue function) revenue can be allocated to the fixed inputs—the effect is similar to that observed earlier when transformation of axes of a polynomial was considered: the fixed factors no longer receive the necessary explicit recognition. If, instead, the fixed factors are incorporated in the constant term,[30] there is an implicit assumption that their only effect on output is to *multiply* the effects of variable inputs—yet there seems no reason from a financial accounting standpoint to make this rather odd assumption.

It is *possible* to select output market functions that, combined with a Cobb-Douglas production function, will yield a homogeneous revenue function. But many

---

in frequency of occurrence, for example losses arising from inventory revaluations; (e) periodical independent costs which are periodical in occurrence but not predictable as to amount, for example additional factory heating expenses depending on the severity of the winter; (f) perfectly fixed costs, or costs of being in business and which could be eliminated only by winding up the firm."

—Vickers (1960) p. 406. The reader will note that many inputs will be fixed even under a strict cash-flows interpretation of the production function. For example, depreciation is eliminated by such an interpretation, but there will be a fixed element in plant replacement.

For fixed elements in what ordinarily are regarded as variable costs, see Julius Wiener, "Separation of Fixed and Variable Costs," *Accounting Review*, XXXV (October, 1960), 686–90.

[27] The simplest and most familiar example of why this is so is the function typically used by accountants to relate *cost* with output:

$$C = a + bU = aU^0 + bU^1$$

where C is cost and U is units of output. This function is nonhomogeneous because the U-term (of degree one) and the constant term (of degree zero) are of different degrees. The constant term results from the presence of fixed factors, in this case fixed costs. Of course it will always be possible to remove fixed factors from a polynomial by transformation of axes. But this results in the fixed inputs no longer receiving explicit recognition in the revenue function, and revenue no longer being allocated to all inputs simultaneously.

[28] Of course other types of production function have been suggested in the economics literature, too. Earlier in this chapter and in the Appendix, a polynomial one mentioned by Allen is used. For an unusually elegant production function, see Arnold Zellner, "An Interesting General Form for a Production Function," *Econometrica*, XIX (April, 1951), 188–89. The author claims that the functional form used also serves as the basis for Planck's Radiation Law.

[29] That is to say, if U represents output, $U=f(A,B,C)$, and C is a fixed input, then output can be expressed by some *other* function $g(A,B)$.

[30] That is, if U represents output, $U=aA^\alpha B^\beta C^\gamma$, and C^γ is fixed, then output can be expressed as $U=bA^\alpha B^\beta$, where a and b are constants.

plausible kinds of market functions will yield nonhomogeneous revenue functions, too (an example is the simple declining-demand market function used in the appendix to this chapter). All in all, it seems difficult to develop a revenue function from a Cobb-Douglas production function and have that revenue function both:

1) incorporate all those features of the firm with which financial accountants must deal, doing so in explicit, plausible ways;
2) be homogeneous.

But it is not claimed that any final conclusions have been reached here. This is an area in which further research would be valuable—especially empirical research at a considerably more detailed level of aggregation than is usually found in the economics literature.

Linear homogeneity

Much the same kind of conclusion must be reached regarding *linear* homogeneity (constant returns to scale) of the revenue function. We already have seen that Hildebrand and Liu uncovered increasing returns to scale in their industry studies. Stigler gives reasons why constant returns to scale are not apt to characterize the firm: the most pertinent of these is that not all inputs are subject to unlimited variation in quantity (entrepreneurship is the most clear-cut example). Increasing returns to scale resulting from more efficient division of labor and use of special purpose machinery in place of general purpose machinery are also possible.[31] Once again, empirical research at the level of aggregation employed in financial accounting would be valuable but it seems likely that even were a revenue function homogeneous it would not be *linear* homogeneous.

The irrelevancy of marginal contributions

But even if the revenue function *is* linear homogeneous, simultaneous allocation by the marginal contributions approach usually will be arbitrary!

The marginal revenue contribution of an input is the increase in total revenues caused by adding one additional unit of that factor. *This concept really applies only to the last unit added.* Under the marginal contributions approach to simultaneous allocation, the marginal revenue contribution of the *last* unit is multiplied by the number of *all* units of the factor employed to obtain the net-revenue contribution of the input:

$$Y_j(t) = M_j(t) \cdot X_j(t)$$

where $Y_j(t)$ represents the net-revenue contribution of input j, $M_j(t)$ the marginal contribution of the last unit of j employed, and $X_j(t)$ the total number of units of j employed.

If the revenue function is linear homogeneous, Euler's Theorem (see the appendix to this chapter) assures us that allocation of the marginal contributions of last units to each of the other units of the same inputs will result in the total revenue being exactly divided up among the various inputs. But this is true only as a kind of arithmetic coincidence. For unless one interprets things in an artificial way, $M_j(t)$

---

[31] See George J. Stigler, *The Theory of Price*, Revised Edition (New York: The Macmillan Company, 1952), pp. 136–40.

is *not* the marginal contribution of any unit of *j* *except* the last one . . . and there is no way to defend the required interpretation against alternative interpretations.

Here is an example. Suppose that a firm employs two inputs, *P* and *Q*, and that the revenue function is the following simple linear homogeneous Cobb-Douglas function (like other examples, this one is not intended to be realistic):

$$Y(t) = P^{\alpha}Q^{1-\alpha}, \qquad \alpha > 0$$

The marginal contributions of the two inputs may be calculated from the following:

$$\frac{\partial Y(t)}{\partial P} = \alpha(P/Q)^{\alpha-1}; \qquad \frac{\partial Y(t)}{\partial Q} = (1-\alpha)(P/Q)^{\alpha}$$

For $P=Q=3$, $Y(t)=3$, and the total marginal contributions do equal the total revenue:

$$\frac{\partial Y(t)}{\partial P} = \alpha; \qquad \frac{\partial Y(t)}{\partial Q} = (1-\alpha)$$

$$Y(t) = 3 = 3\alpha + 3(1-\alpha)$$

But did each of the three units of *Q* contribute the same amount to revenue? Suppose we imagine the firm as initially employing 3 units of *P* and one of *Q*, then add units of *Q* until the firm is employing 3 units of each. The following table gives the contribution to revenue of each additional unit of *Q*:

Number of Q Used	Contribution of Last Unit
1	$(1-\alpha)\,(3/1)^{\alpha}$
2	$(1-\alpha)\,(3/2)^{\alpha}$
3	$(1-\alpha)\,(3/3)^{\alpha}=(1-\alpha)$

Clearly, the contribution to revenue of the last unit employed changes with the increase in the number of units of *Q* employed. Why would one wish to allocate the same amount of revenue to each unit of *Q*? Yet this is exactly what the marginal approach does in the equation:

$$Y_j(t) = M_j(t) \cdot X_j(t)$$

The contributions of all units employed will be the same *only* if during the expansion process from one unit to three units of *Q* the ratio *P/Q* is equal to unity at each step of the expansion process. This requires starting with one unit of each kind of input, then simultaneously adding second units of each, then third units of each— in other words, it requires simultaneous successive expansion. The assumption of simultaneous successive expansion is an arbitrary one—because any of a variety of alternative assumptions could be made, and there would be no way to defend the choice of simultaneous successive expansion against these alternatives. The only kinds of revenue functions for which marginal contributions allocations will *not* be arbitrary are simple additive functions—ones without interaction terms. And, as we have already seen, for functions of this kind marginal contributions allocation isn't *necessary*—simple additive allocation will suffice.

Another example

I conclude with another argument that also points up the irrelevancy of the marginal contributions approach to the problem of determining the input's contribution to revenues. Suppose that the revenue function is the following linear homogeneous function, with A a depreciable asset and B some other kind of input. Also, suppose that this is the revenue function for each year of the service lives of the A-assets.

$$Y(t) = \frac{10AB - A^2 - 5B^2}{A + B}$$

At $A = 30$, $B = 10$ the total revenue will be \$40. But, as the reader can verify, at (30, 10) the marginal contributions of the B's are \$4 and the A's are \$0! Since the Euler's Theorem assumptions are satisfied, total revenue *is* exactly allocated to the inputs:

$$Y(t) = \$40 = 30(\$0) + 10(\$4) = A\frac{\partial Y(t)}{\partial A} + B\frac{\partial Y(t)}{\partial B}$$

But the allocation is obviously nonsensical (how can the *depreciation* allocation be performed for asset A if the contributions allocation results in a zero contribution in each year of its life?) The only reason that this particular allocation occurs is that the last unit of asset A acquired happened to have a marginal contribution of zero. This is unrealistic, but it is in an extreme case like this that the arbitrariness of employing the marginal contribution of the last unit to determine the total contribution of the group becomes obvious.

The same misuse of the marginal contribution of the last unit, pushed one step further, results in the nonsensical phenomenon of negative assets. Suppose for instance that 31 A were used and 10 B. The results would be as follows:[32]

Kind of Input	Marginal Contribution	Number of Units Used	Total
A..................	$-81/(41)^2$	31	$\$-2,511/(41)^2$
B..................	$6,971/(41)^2$	10	$69,710/(41)^2$
Total...			$\$\ 67,199/(41)^2 = \$1,639/41$
Revenue...			$\$\ \ \ 1,639/41$

[32] The reduced figures are as follows:

Kind of Input	Marginal Contribution	Number of Units Used	Total
A..................	$\$-0.0482$	31	$\$-\ \ 1.49$
B..................	4.147	10	41.47
Total...			$\$\ \ 39.98$
Revenue...			$\$\ \ 39.98$

The revenue function is linear homogeneous. A's are necessary for there to be any revenue at all (at $A = 0$ the function is negative for any positive value of B). Yet the marginal contributions approach results in the A's being treated as making a negative group contribution to revenues merely because the marginal contribution of the *last* unit is negative. The arbitrariness of using the marginal contribution of the last unit in this way is obvious in this case. The marginal contributions approach is equally arbitrary in any other case (and for the same reasons), although the results may *appear* plausible under more realistic circumstances. The only exception, once again, will be in cases where there is a simple additive revenue function.

Summary

The simultaneous-allocation form of the net-revenue-contributions approach requires a contributions allocation in which total estimated revenues in each year are allocated to all the inputs generating them. There is no set of rules upon which laymen would agree for performing this allocation. Economic theory suggests three approaches which might be used to justify this simultaneous contributions allocation. It is possible that other approaches may be developed in the future, but these are the only ones available *now*:

1. Simple additive allocation—it was shown that this approach cannot be justified if the revenue function incorporates input interactions.

2. Linear activity analysis—it was shown that this approach requires assumptions (including interaction assumptions) that usually will not fit the nature of the phenomena faced by the financial accountant.

3. Marginal contributions allocation—it was shown (in the text and in the appendix) that this approach cannot be theoretically justified unless the revenue function is linear homogeneous. It was argued (but not demonstrated conclusively) that linear homogeneity will not usually characterize the kinds of revenue functions faced by accountants. However, it was also shown that even when the revenue function *is* linear homogeneous, marginal contributions allocation cannot be theoretically justified unless the revenue function is simple additive.

Therefore, it may be concluded that the simultaneous allocation form of the net-revenue-contributions approach cannot presently be given theoretical justification except with simple additive revenue functions. Since the assumption of simple additivity implies no input interactions, this conclusion may be restated as follows:

The simultaneous-allocation form of the net-revenue contributions approach can presently be given theoretical justification only when the firm's inputs do not interact.

Since, as we have seen, there is extensive input interaction in most firms, this is tantamount to saying that in most cases the simultaneous-allocation form of the net-revenue-contributions approach is arbitrary. It should be emphasized that this conclusion applies only to the *present* state of allocation theory. No assertion is made that theoretical justification of such allocations is impossible. At any time, someone may invent a new approach to allocation under which simultaneous allocation could be theoretically justified. But in the typical case no such approach exists now.

Appendix

Homogeneity[33]

Homogeneity is a property of functions. A function is an unambiguous rule for associating members of one set with members of another set. For example, the function $f(X) = X^3$ associates the X-value 2 with the function-value 8, the X-value -10 with the function-value $-1,000$, and so forth. The function:

$$f(A, B) = \frac{15AB - 5A^2 - 4B^2}{A + B}$$

associates the *pair* of A- and B-values (6, 7) with the function-value 19.54, the pair (10, 10) with the function-value 30.00, and so forth.

Consider the first of these functions, $f(X) = X^3$. Suppose that we pick a constant, k, and multiply every X-value by it. Doing so will generate new X-values. These will be associated with new function-values. A function will be *homogeneous* if the follow-

---

[33] The following is a very brief discussion of the mathematical property of homogeneity and its bearing on allocation of net-revenue contributions. I have discussed this property elsewhere—see Thomas (1964), and Arthur L. Thomas, *Revenue Recognition* (Ann Arbor, Michigan: University of Michigan, 1966), pp. 104–20. I use the same main illustration here that is used there, but have omitted the details of certain calculations. The basic mathematical proposition involved in this discussion is Euler's Theorem. A general mathematical background will be found in R. G. D. Allen, *Mathematical Analysis for Economists* (New York: Macmillan Co., 1939), pp. 315–22; and Taro Yamane, *Mathematics for Economists* (Englewood Cliffs, New Jersey: Prentice-Hall, 1962), pp. 90–100, 127–29. The basic production function used below is one mentioned in Allen (1939) p. 322:

$$U = \frac{aAB - bA^2 - cB^2}{dA + eB}$$

—where U represents output, A and B represent the numbers of units employed of two different kinds of inputs, and lower case letters represent positive constants. This kind of production function provides another example of why a contributions allocation that looks only to the separate effects of the inputs is arbitrary. In production functions of this form, both of the separate effects will be negative—even when total output is positive! (Notice that this phenomenon of negative separate effects is entirely different from the phenomenon of negative marginal contributions discussed toward the end of Chapter Three. Negative marginal contributions will characterize only certain values of A and B; negative separate effects characterize *all* positive values of A and B. Negative separate effects are a familiar phenomenon in everyday life; examples include the separate effects of garlic or pepper in a recipe, and the separate effects of an automobile considered apart from its brakes—as known through the effects of driving an automobile that *lacks* brakes.) A little experimentation should convince the reader that this phenomenon will occur for at least *some* essential inputs over a wide variety of plausible polynomial functions.

Euler's Theorem is easily stated. Assume that the function:

$$Z = f(x_1, x_2, \cdots, x_m)$$

is homogeneous—that is, that for any constant, k:

$$f(kx_1, kx_2, \cdots, kx_m) = k^n f(x_1, x_2, \cdots, x_m)$$

where n is an exponent. Then, according to Euler's Theorem:

$$x_1 \frac{\partial Z}{\partial x_1} + x_2 \frac{\partial Z}{\partial x_2} + \cdots + x_m \frac{\partial Z}{\partial x_m} = nf(x_1, x_2, \cdots, x_m)$$

There is an elementary discussion of production functions, Euler's Theorem, and the marginal-contributions approach to allocation in Jean E. Draper and Jane S. Klingman, *Mathematical Analysis: Business and Economic Applications* (New York: Harper & Row, Publishers, 1967), pp. 298–303. However, there is a typographical error in their discussion that might prove confusing: the equation on the top of page 300 reads $x(\partial x/\partial z)$, when it should read $x(\partial z/\partial x)$.

ing is true of each new function-value, $f(kX)$:

$$f(kX) = k^n f(X)$$

where n is an exponent. Such a function is called *homogeneous of degree n.* For example, $f(X) = X^3$ is homogeneous of degree 3, since:

$$f(kX) = k^3 X^3 = k^3 f(X)$$

The function $f(A,B)$ is homogeneous of degree 1, since

$$f(kA, kB) = \frac{15kAkB - 5k^2 A^2 - 4k^2 B^2}{kA + kB}$$

$$= \left[\frac{k^2}{k}\right]\left[\frac{15AB - 5A^2 - 4B^2}{A + B}\right] = kf(A, B)$$

Many functions are *not* homogeneous. For instance, the function $f(Y) = a + bY$ is not homogeneous, since:

$$f(kY) = a + bkY = k \cdot \left[\frac{a}{k} + bY\right]$$

and there is no way in which the latter expression can be converted into one having the form $k^n f(Y)$. As another example, $f(Y,Z) = 7Y + YZ$ is not homogeneous, since:

$$f(kY, kZ) = 7kY + kYkZ = k(7Y) + k^2(YZ)$$

and there is no way to convert this latter expression to one having the form $k^n f(Y,Z)$. Call such functions *nonhomogeneous.*

The degree of a polynomial term[34]

Under what conditions will a function be homogeneous? We can answer this for polynomials if we introduce another notion: the "degree" of a term. Consider the term:

$$aX_1^{n1} X_2^{n2} \cdots X_m^{nm}$$

where a is a constant, the X's are variables, and the n's are exponents. This term will have the degree d, where $d = (n1 + n2 + \cdots + nm)$. For instance, the terms X^2 and XY are both of degree 2; the terms X^3, X^2Y, and XYZ are all of degree 3; and so forth.

For a polynomial to be homogeneous, its terms must all be of the same degree.[35] For example, $15AB - 5A^2 - 4B^2$ is homogeneous—all of its terms are of degree 2. For a *ratio* of polynomials to be homogeneous, all of the terms in each polynomial must be of the same degree, though the degree may differ between the two polynomials. For example, the function:

---

[34] The material in this subsection goes beyond the discussion of homogeneity in Thomas (1966). That discussion reached some of its tentative conclusions by a kind of trial-and-error experimentation with production and market functions. The matters discussed here help explain why these experiments yielded the results that they did.

[35] See A. Adrian Albert, *Introduction to Algebraic Theories* (Chicago: University of Chicago Press, 1941), pp. 6–8, for homogeneous polynomials. The discussion there is easily extended to ratios of polynomials.

$$f(A, B) = \frac{15AB - 5A^2 - 4B^2}{A + B}$$

is a ratio of polynomials. All terms in the numerator are of degree 2; all terms in the denominator are of degree 1. Therefore $f(A,B)$ is homogeneous. For ease of exposition, this kind of situation will be described as one in which *all polynomial terms are of the same degree.* But the reader might keep in mind that the requirement for ratios of polynomials is not quite this severe.

Allocation of revenue to two or more kinds of inputs

Suppose that two or more different kinds of inputs are jointly employed in earning revenue. For simplicity, assume that these inputs are machines: A-machines and B-machines, and that they produce a single product. Let U be the number of units of this product produced. Suppose that the firm's production function is:

$$U = f(A, B) = \frac{15AB - 5A^2 - 4B^2}{A + B}$$

Finally, suppose that any product produced is immediately sold for $1.00 a unit. Then $f(A, B)$ is also the firm's *revenue* function. Notice that this revenue function incorporates an interaction effect in its $15AB$ term.

According to this revenue function, if we use 6 A-machines and 7 B-machines the revenue will be $19.54. If we use 10 A's and 10 B's the revenue will be $30.00 and so forth. Suppose that we do the latter and want to know how much of this $30.00 should be considered to be the contribution of each kind of machine. Using the marginal contributions approach that is discussed in the body of this study, we get the following result:[36]

Kind of Machine	Marginal Contribution	Number of Machines Used	Total
A..............	$1.00	10	$10.00
B..............	2.00	10	20.00
Revenue...			$30.00

[36] As an example, the calculation of the marginal contribution associated with an A-machine is illustrated. We know from elementary calculus that:

$$\frac{d(u/v)}{dx} = \frac{v\frac{du}{dx} - u\frac{dv}{dx}}{v^2}, \text{ and that } \frac{d(u + v)}{dx} = \frac{du}{dx} + \frac{dv}{dx}; \text{ so,}$$

$$\frac{\partial f}{\partial A}[f(A, B)] = \frac{\left[(A + B)\left(\frac{\partial f}{\partial A}(15AB - 5A^2 - 4B^2)\right)\right] - \left[(15AB - 5A^2 - 4B^2)\left(\frac{\partial f}{\partial A}(A + B)\right)\right]}{(A + B)^2}$$

$$= \frac{[(A + B)(15B - 10A)] - [(15AB - 5A^2 - 4B^2)(1)]}{(A + B)^2}$$

Substituting $A = 10$ and $B = 10$, we obtain the following for the marginal contribution associated with one A-machine:

$$\frac{[(10 + 10)(150 - 100)] - [(1,500 - 500 - 400)]}{(20)^2} = \frac{(20 \times 50) - 600}{400} = \frac{400}{400} = 1.00.$$

The $30.00 revenue has been exactly allocated to the twenty machines employed in earning it, according to the marginal contribution made by each kind of machine. The revenue function $f(A, B)$ is homogeneous of degree one, or *linear* homogeneous. Though it is argued toward the end of Chapter Three that the allocation is an arbitrary one, it will always be possible to perform this kind of allocation (despite the presence of interaction effects) as long as the revenue function is linear homogeneous. (The problem of functions homogeneous of degrees *other* than one will be discussed at the end of this Appendix.) But this will not usually be true if the revenue function is *non*homogeneous. If the revenue function is nonhomogeneous, allocation usually can be shown to be arbitrary without recourse to any of the arguments presented at the end of Chapter Three.

This is easily demonstrated by changing $f(A, B)$ so that it no longer is homogeneous, then seeing what happens. One way to do this is to change one of the terms in the numerator so that it no longer is of degree 2. Suppose that $15AB$ is changed to A^2B, giving the nonhomogeneous revenue function:

$$g(A, B) = \frac{A^2B - 5A^2 - 4B^2}{A + B}$$

Assume that again we use 10 A's and 10 B's. Solving for these values, we find that revenue will be $5.00. Calculating marginal contributions in the same way as before, we get the following results:

Kind of Machine	Marginal Contribution	Number of Machines Used	Total
A..............	$4.75	10	$47.50
B..............	0.75	10	7.50
Total..			$55.00
Revenue..			$ 5.00

The total of the marginal contributions is eleven times as much as the revenue! If we were to insist upon allocating according to the marginal contributions there are various ways in which we could do so. We might allocate 1/11th dollar of revenue for each dollar of marginal contributions. But this implicitly assumes that each machine is equally "responsible" for the $50.00 discrepancy. Were anyone to recommend some other way to adjust the marginal contributions to the revenue, there is nothing in economic theory (and no rule to which laymen would agree) that would bar the alternative. For example, why not charge $2.50 of the "extra" contribution to each machine? To be sure, this makes the contributions of the B-machines negative; but as the next example will show, this is a common result anyway. The $50 could also be employed in creating a kind of valuation account for the firm's depreciable assets as a whole.

Any allocation here in terms of marginal contributions is unable to defend itself against alternate allocation patterns; so any such allocation is arbitrary. It is arbitrary for another reason, too: we have no idea in advance of how the allocation is to be performed; we must employ some after-the-fact rule, in much the same way as that in which defenders of the Ptolemaic system of astronomy had to apply a series of after-the-fact patches to incorporate new data about the planets.

Homogeneity at a point

Nonhomogeneous functions do not *invariably* run into these difficulties. A function can be generally nonhomogeneous, and yet at a point have the characteristic of homogeneity (in the sense that the marginal contributions exactly equal the total revenue at that point). Euler's Theorem implies that when the revenue function is linear homogeneous, the equality of total marginal contributions and revenue holds as an *identity*; however, it can hold as an *equation* when the function is nonhomogeneous (though it need not do so). For example:

$$\bar{g}(A, B) = \frac{A^2B - 5A^2 - 4B^2}{A + B} + 50$$

is generally nonhomogeneous, but homogeneous at the point (10, 10). Typically, though, if the revenue function is nonhomogeneous, allocation will be arbitrary.[37]

Another example

Here is another, slightly more complicated, example of nonhomogeneous revenue functions. We have assumed up to now that any product produced is immediately sold for $1.00 per unit. This allowed us to treat the production function $f(A, B)$ as also being the firm's revenue function. We can obtain another nonhomogeneous revenue function by assuming that there is a declining demand for additional units of the firm's product. One of the simplest market functions meeting this condition would be:

$$P = 2.00 - 0.01U$$

where P is the unit selling price that the firm can obtain for its product, and U (as before) is the number of units of product produced and sold. Combining the production and market functions gives us a new revenue function

$$h(A, B) = f(A, B) \cdot [2.00 - 0.01f(A, B)]$$

When expanded, this turns out to be a relatively complicated, nonhomogeneous polynomial function which reaches its maximum of $42.43 when 6 A-machines and 7 B-machines are employed. Calculating marginal contributions, we get the following results:

Kind of Machine	Marginal Contribution	Number of Machines Used	Total
A................	$0.226	6	$ 1.36
B...............	(0.083)	7	(0.58)
Total...			$ 0.78
Revenue...			$42.43

---

[37] It can be argued that if the revenue function is not homogeneous (in this sense) at the point at which the firm is operating, then the firm is not maximizing revenues. But failure to maximize revenues is a common enough phenomenon.

Here, marginal contributions are less than 1/54th of the revenue. Once again, any allocation of the revenue in terms of the marginal contributions will be unable to be defended against alternate allocation patterns. In conclusion, homogeneity of *some* degree is an essential implicit requirement if the marginal contributions approach is to yield theoretically justified allocations.

Homogeneity of degrees other than one[38]

But what about functions that are *non*linear homogeneous, homogeneous of degrees other than one? Here is a revenue function similar to our original $f(A, B)$, but which is homogeneous of degree two:

$$Y(t) = \frac{66AB - 4A^2 - 2B^2}{200}$$

Assuming that we again use 10 of each kind of machine, revenue will be $30.00. But total marginal contributions will be *twice* revenue:

Kind of Machine	Marginal Contribution	Number of Machines Used	Total
A...............	$2.90	10	$29.00
B...............	3.10	10	31.00
Total...			$60.00
Revenue...			$30.00

In general, Euler's Theorem implies that whenever the revenue function is homogeneous of degree k, the total of the marginal contributions will be k times the revenue. In such cases, the revenue can always be allocated by multiplying each of the marginal contributions by $1/k$; that is:

$$Y(t) = \frac{A}{k} \cdot \frac{\partial f(A, B)}{\partial A} + \frac{B}{k} \cdot \frac{\partial f(A, B)}{\partial B}$$

whenever $f(A, B)$ is homogeneous of degree k. But why is this adjustment any less arbitrary than was multiplying the marginal contributions by 1/11 in the nonhomogeneous case? The only difference is that we know *in advance* about multiplying by $1/k$. Otherwise, aren't exactly the same kinds of alternatives open here as were available in the nonhomogeneous case? For example, we equally well know in advance that the total discrepancy will be $kY(t) - Y(t) = (k\text{-}1) \cdot Y(t)$. If a total of m machines were to be employed, we could charge (or credit, depending on sign) $[(k-1) \cdot Y(t)]/m$ against the marginal contribution of each machine. The $1/k$ adjustment gives adjusted marginal contributions of $1.45 and $1.55 to the A and B-machines, respectively; this adjustment would give adjusted contributions of $1.40 and $1.60.

---

[38] The reader should be warned that I have twice changed my mind on the matters discussed in this subsection. In Thomas (1964), pp. 7–8 it was argued that if the revenue function was non-linear homogeneous, allocations using the marginal contributions approach would be arbitrary. Professor Harold Bierman, Jr., was kind enough to initiate a correspondence in which he argued that this position was incorrect. His arguments seemed convincing, and were summarized in Thomas (1966), p. 113n (they are repeated in what follows). However, I have now returned to my 1964 position, for reasons that are also given below.

Other alternative ways of adjusting the marginal contributions are known in advance, too; there is nothing sacred in the constant k.

For that matter, *any* revenue function, whether or not homogeneous, will at any point have the characteristic that there is *some* constant k such that k times the total marginal contributions will equal the revenue. If the function is homogeneous, k will always be the same at any point; but this is insufficient reason to claim that multiplying the marginal contributions by $1/k$ is preferable to any other allocation approach: even in the *non*homogeneous case the *formula* for k is the same at any point . . . you just don't know the *number* in advance. This is easily demonstrated:[39]

Suppose that the revenue function for Year t is the nonhomogeneous function given below, where $Y(t)$ is the revenue in Year t; P and Q are the numbers of units of two different kinds of inputs used in Year t; n, m, r, and s are exponents; and c_1 and c_2 are constants:

$$Y(t) = f(P, Q) = c_1 P^n Q^m + c_2 P^r Q^s \qquad (n + m \neq r + s)$$

Let $A = c_1 P^n Q^m$, and $B = c_2 P^r Q^s$. It can be proven that the following relationship always will prevail between the total revenues for Year t and the marginal contributions of the two kinds of inputs:

$$Y(t) = P\left[\frac{1}{m+n} \cdot \frac{\partial A}{\partial P} + \frac{1}{r+s} \cdot \frac{\partial B}{\partial P}\right] + Q\left[\frac{1}{m+n} \cdot \frac{\partial A}{\partial Q} + \frac{1}{r+s} \cdot \frac{\partial B}{\partial Q}\right]$$

$$= f\left[\frac{\partial Y(t)}{\partial P}, \frac{\partial Y(t)}{\partial Q}\right]$$

Proof:

$$\frac{\partial A}{\partial P} = nc_1 P^{n-1} Q^m \qquad \frac{\partial B}{\partial P} = rc_2 P^{r-1} Q^s$$

$$\frac{\partial A}{\partial Q} = mc_1 P^n Q^{m-1} \qquad \frac{\partial B}{\partial Q} = sc_2 P^r Q^{s-1}$$

$$f\left[\frac{\partial Y(t)}{\partial P}, \frac{\partial Y(t)}{\partial Q}\right] = P\left[\frac{nc_1 P^{n-1} Q^m}{m+n} + \frac{rc_2 P^{r-1} Q^s}{r+s}\right] + Q\left[\frac{mc_1 P^n Q^{m-1}}{m+n} + \frac{sc_2 P^r Q^{s-1}}{r+s}\right]$$

$$= P\left[\frac{n(r+s)c_1 P^{n-1} Q^m + r(m+n)c_2 P^{r-1} Q^s}{(m+n)(r+s)}\right]$$

$$\quad + Q\left[\frac{m(r+s)c_1 P^n Q^{m-1} + s(m+n)c_2 P^r Q^{s-1}}{(m+n)(r+s)}\right]$$

$$= \frac{n(r+s)c_1 P^n Q^m + r(m+n)c_2 P^r Q^s + m(r+s)c_1 P^n Q^m + s(m+n)c_2 P^r Q^s}{(m+n)(r+s)}$$

$$= \frac{(m+n)(r+s)c_1 P^n Q^m + (m+n)(r+s)c_2 P^r Q^s}{(m+n)(r+s)}$$

$$= c_1 P^n Q^m + c_2 P^r Q^s = f(P, Q) = Y(t)$$

---

[39] I am indebted to Professor Lawrence A. Sherr for the following demonstration.

The foregoing may, of course, be generalized to cover any desired number of different kinds of inputs, keeping in mind, though, that the result applies only to polynomials of the form illustrated. If Euler's Theorem provides a theoretical basis for allocation when $m+n=r+s\neq1$, (for a nonlinear homogeneous function), then the above provides a theoretical basis for allocation when $m+n\neq r+s$ (for a nonhomogeneous function). Since we have already seen that allocations in the latter case are arbitrary, it follows that allocations in the nonlinear homogeneous case will be arbitrary, too.

Of course, by similar logic it also could be argued that there is nothing sacred about the constant 1, either—that is, that allocation in the *linear* homogeneous case is arbitrary, too. But this conclusion is reached in Chapter Three by another route.

CHAPTER FOUR

Net-Revenue Contributions: The Capital-Budgeting Approach

THE net-revenue-contributions approach requires estimating the effect of the depreciable asset on the firm's future revenues or costs. In the last chapter we saw that two allocations were required: a *contributions* allocation, in which net revenues are allocated to inputs; then a *depreciation* allocation, in which the results of the contributions allocation are employed in allocating the acquisition price of the depreciable asset. The contributions allocation can be performed in two ways:

1. *The simultaneous-allocation approach.* This requires that in each year the total estimated *revenues* be allocated to *all* inputs simultaneously. This is the approach that was discussed in the last chapter.

2. *The capital-budgeting approach.* This requires that the sequence of the firm's *net income* (gross of the depreciation of the asset) be estimated on two different assumptions:

   a) that the asset had not been acquired (designated as $Z^0(t)$ in year t)

   b) that the asset had been acquired and used (designated as $Z'(t)$ in year t)

In each year, t, the asset's net-revenue contribution is regarded as equal to $Z'(t) - Z^0(t)$, that is, as equal to the difference between the net income from the second and first sequences (the algebraic notation employed here was developed early in Chapter Three). Sequential analysis is thereby substituted for the simultaneous analysis employed in Chapter Three. This is the approach that is discussed in this chapter.

Depreciable assets are not purchased simultaneously. They are purchased one at a time. This suggests a possible way out of our earlier difficulties. Perhaps one could determine the asset's net-revenue contributions by examining the capital budgeting estimates made at the time it was purchased. Such data are available, and this approach *seems* to avoid the entire problem of interactions by refusing to look at more than one asset in any one set of calculations. A note in Chapter Two (on the evolution of the net-revenue-contributions approach) listed various examples of the capital-budgeting approach. Here are two influential ones from the literature:

In our approach, the depreciation pattern is determined at the same time as the decision is taken to acquire assets that depreciate. The depreciation for any period thus derived is then matched with the actual revenues of that period. Outlay, also, is on an actual basis. If the outcome in any one period is better than was expected, there will be an excess on net income, which will be duly recognized. If the outcome is worse than was expected, then a short fall in net income (perhaps even a loss) will be reported. Thus, there will be no arbitrary smoothing of the curve of profits.[1]

As long as expectations do not change, periodic estimates of depreciation should be consistent with the pattern of service expirations anticipated at the time of acquisition.

---

[1] Hector R. Anton, "Depreciation, Cost Allocation and Investment Decisions," *Accounting Research*, VII (April, 1956), 122. Two other early and influential articles were Isaac N. Reynolds, "Selecting the Proper Depreciation Method," *Accounting Review*, XXXVI (April, 1961), 239–48; and Harold Bierman, Jr., "Depreciable Assets—Timing of Expense Recognition," *Accounting Review*, XXXVI (October, 1961), 613–18.

... The formula utilized should be designed to yield depreciation estimates that roughly parallel the expected service pattern, even though this may be determined only within very broad limits.[2]

An illustration

The capital-budgeting approach will be illustrated by modifying an earlier example. Suppose for simplicity that a company employs only two kinds of inputs, P-machines and Q-machines, and that its income function (gross of depreciation) is the same in all years under consideration:[3]

$$Z = 20P - P^2 + 3PQ + 13Q - 6Q^2$$

where Z represents net income gross of depreciation, and P and Q are the numbers of P-machines and Q-machines employed. The reader should note that this income function is nonhomogeneous and incorporates an interaction effect.

Suppose that at the beginning of Year 1 only P-machines were available to the firm, that they cost \$30 apiece, and that they had service lives of 4 years. With no Q-machines, we may substitute $Q = 0$ into the previous income function to obtain:

$$Z^0 = 20P - P^2$$

—the first income sequence (in which it is assumed that the asset—the Q-machines in this case—had not been acquired). Suppose that the firm purchased six P-machines at the beginning of Year 1; then $Z^0 = 120 - 36 = \$84$. Finally, suppose that at the *end* of Year 1, Q-machines became available for the first time, cost \$34 apiece, have service lives of three years,[4] and that the company buys two of them. The income in each of the three remaining years of P-machine estimated service life will be \$38 per year higher as a result of acquiring and using the Q-machines:

$$Z = 20P - P^2 + 3PQ + 13Q - 6Q^2$$
$$Z' = 120 - 36 + 36 + 26 - 24 \dots\dots\dots\dots\dots \$122.00$$
$$Z^0 = 120 - 36 + 0 + 0 - 0 \dots\dots\dots\dots\dots 84.00$$

Estimated net-revenue contributions of the Q-machines $\$ 38.00$[5]

The implicit interest rate of the investment in the Q-machines turns out to be 31.06 percent. The depreciation allocation for the two Q-machines is shown in Table 4–1.

Clearly, one could argue, the decision to buy two Q-machines had incremental effects on net income (gross of depreciation) of \$38 a year for three years. These incremental effects can be readily identified *even though the income function incorpo-*

[2] American Accounting Association Committee on Concepts and Standards—Long-Lived Assets, "Accounting for Lánd, Buildings, and Equipment," *Accounting Review*, XXXIX (July, 1964), 696–97. The appropriate response to *changed* expectations will be discussed later in this chapter.

[3] So that $Z^0(1) = Z^0(2) = Z^0(3) = Z^0(4) = Z^0$, and $Z'(1) = Z'(2) = Z'(3) = Z'(4) = Z'$. In this example, the Q-machine plays the role of asset j.

[4] This assumption of three-year service lives for the Q-machines is made only for simplicity—this way the P-machines' and Q-machines' services are exhausted on the same date.

[5] Technically, to agree with the earlier description of the capital-budgeting approach, both Z' and Z^0 should be gross of depreciation of the Q-machines, but *net* of depreciation of the P-machines: that is, both Z' and Z^0 should have the appropriate amount of P-machine depreciation subtracted from the figures \$122 and \$84. But this does not affect the calculation of the estimated contributions of the Q-machines and, for simplicity, will therefore be ignored here and elsewhere in the discussion.

rates interaction effects and is nonhomogeneous, and can be used to defend what turns out to be an increasing-charge depreciation pattern for the two Q-machines. In general, it can be argued that any time one buys new depreciable assets one may look at the capital-budgeting calculations supporting this decision. These calculations are based upon estimates of the effects of purchasing the new assets on the net incomes of future years. These can be used to defend a depreciation pattern for the new assets.[6]

TABLE 4-1

CALCULATION OF ANNUAL DEPRECIATION FOR TWO Q-MACHINES

Year	(A) Current Year Rate of Return	(B) Investment (Beginning-of-Year Book Value)	(C) Appropriate Earnings for Year ($A \times B$)	(D) Estimated Net-Revenue Contributions	Depreciation for the Year ($D - C$)
2.........	31.06%	$68.00	$21.12	$38.00	$16.88
3.........	31.06	51.12	15.88	38.00	22.12
4.........	31.06	29.00	9.00	38.00	29.00
Total..					$68.00

Changes in estimates

Of course, once they are purchased the new assets merge with the previously owned assets. Assuming that the income function incorporates interaction effects, the new assets simply become part of the total set of inputs that jointly generate income.[7] Suppose that, subsequent to the purchase, the accountant again revises his estimates of what future net income will be. Perhaps still another kind of machine becomes available, purchase of which would further improve net income. This is essentially what happened after the purchase of the *P*-machines in the previous example. It should be evident that when estimates change in this way one cannot theoretically justify recalculation of depreciation on the previously owned assets. The capital-budgeting approach automatically assigns the *whole* change in estimated income to the new assets. *Doing so is exactly what keeps the capital-budgeting approach seemingly free of the interaction problems discussed in Chapter Three.* When new assets are purchased, *none* of the incremental income is associated with the old assets. Since (under the capital-budgeting approach) the depreciation pattern is determined by allocating 100 percent of the incremental income to the new assets, there is no incremental in-

---

[6] The following point is not germane to the central argument, but still is worth making. Much of the plausibility of the capital-budgeting approach depends on one's underlying belief that firms *should* make capital budgeting estimates. But often it may instead be preferable to use a simulation model for a particular decision. This simulation model need not yield the data necessary for the depreciation allocation, in which case arguments for the capital-budgeting approach are thrown into disarray.

[7] Canning said much the same thing in 1929:

"But the condition of independent, or primary, valuing of the service unit *in terms of money* can be fulfilled when, and only when, those services *are separately to be exchanged for money*. To the extent that a price per unit of service, whether for all or part of the service, can be rationally forecast we can value directly. But the items under consideration are those not to be sold or rented but to be used in conjunction with others for the making of a product that is to be sold. In a plant in which tractors are manufactured for sale, how much of the service of bringing in the dollar-receipts from a given sale is attributable to coal burned under the boilers, how much to the service of the boiler, how much to the various devices in foundry, machine shop, assembly floor, how much to the firemen, moulders, machinists, and night watchmen?"

—John B. Canning, *The Economics of Accountancy* (New York: The Ronald Press Company, 1929), pp. 232–33.

come "left over" for use in altering the depreciation patterns of old assets. So the depreciation patterns for previously owned assets must be left unchanged when a new asset is acquired.[8] More generally, once the depreciation pattern for an asset has been determined by the capital-budgeting approach, changes in the accountant's estimates of future revenues or cost savings cannot be used to change that depreciation pattern without becoming enmeshed in the ambiguities of the simultaneous allocation approach.[9]

Significance of the balance sheet

Though the capital-budgeting approach avoids the direct effects of the interaction problem, it does so at a price: the figures that the accountant reports acquire strange meanings.

First of all, it is important to recognize that the illustrations in this chapter have been highly simplified. Few companies employ just two kinds of inputs. Our illustrations have been confined to machines; actually, as we have seen, the inputs of any firm also include different kinds of labor and various other single-year economic goods. While we may be able to speak unambiguously of the effects of the *decision to buy* new machines on future net income, we should be aware that these effects are joint effects of that decision on *all* inputs. The productivity of previously owned assets changes when a new asset is purchased. So does the productivity of labor and other goods which are not reported as assets. If the income function incorporates interaction effects (as we have seen it almost always will), the *individual* productivity changes will not add up to the total change in product, for reasons given in Chapter Three. This leaves us with a dilemma. We can easily enough say that *total* entity productivity, the *total* entity situation, has been improved by the decision to buy the asset. But if we wish to decompose this improvement into its components, we must recognize that many of these components will be interaction effects. While it is true that the productivity improvement relates to the new asset, it relates equally as much to all *other* inputs. There is no theoretically justified way to allocate these interaction effects to the individual inputs—for the same reasons that, in Chapter Three, we saw that simultaneous allocation must be arbitrary if interaction effects are present. As Chapter One pointed out, an allocation that looks only to the separate effects and ignores the interaction effects will be arbitrary, too—if only because it treats the individual inputs

---

[8] If one wishes to change the patterns of two or more assets, one also gets into problems (discussed later in this chapter) of the *order* in which assets are examined. Contrast the positions taken in T. N. Young and C. G. Peirson, "Depreciation—Future Services Basis," *Accounting Review*, XLII (April, 1967), 339–40; and Richard P. Brief and Joel Owen, "Depreciation and Capital Gains: A 'New' Approach," *Accounting Review*, XLIII (April, 1968), 367–72. The AAA Committee on Long-Lived Assets seems implicitly to allow changes in depreciation patterns for previously-owned assets; see AAA (Land), p. 696.

[9] The merging of depreciable assets, once purchased, into the totality of company inputs parallels the merging of individual lots of a fungible good into a larger inventory of that good. A simple example should make this parallel clear. Suppose that an investor purchased 100 shares of a particular stock in 1937 at $5 a share, then purchased another 100 shares of the same company in 1966 for $100 a share. Assume that there were no stock dividends or splits. Finally, suppose that in 1969 the investor sells 100 shares for $80 a share. Depending upon which shares he prefers to sell, this investor may report anywhere from a $7,500 gain to a $2,000 loss on the 1969 sale. Yet his final economic position is the same (except for tax effects) whichever he reports.

This ambiguity arises in part because once the 1966 shares were purchased they effectively merged, blended, with the other, previously owned, shares. (The ambiguity also, of course, arises in part from our unwillingness to report current costs—see Robert T. Sprouse, "Historical Costs and Current Assets—Traditional and Treacherous," *Accounting Review* XXXVIII (October, 1963), 687–95, and especially pp. 691–692). A similar ambiguity is involved in speaking of the net-revenue contributions of an individual asset once it has joined previously owned assets. In effect, if the income function incorporates interactions, the assets merge into a totality.

as though they were divested of the firm. Therefore, we are left with two alternatives:
1. Give explicit recognition to interaction effects as distinct inputs;
2. Recognize only the improvement in the *total* entity situation resulting from the decision to buy the asset—that is, don't try to allocate the productivity improvement.

The first possibility has been mentioned by Bodenhorn, who speaks of possibly reporting interaction terms on the balance sheet.[10] These interaction terms would be positive or negative, depending on whether the combination of inputs produced more or less product than the inputs would individually; presumably most interactions would be positive.

But consider the number of different kinds of inputs to the firm—including the number that at present are not even reflected on the balance sheet. Consider the number of possible two, three, . . . , *n*-input interactions. Consider also that it would be necessary to allocate all of the interaction effects to the activities of one or more years (some would be single-year effects, but presumably some would be multi-year). The first step in this allocation would be to divide up the asset's acquisition price into a portion applicable to the asset's separate effects and portions applicable to its various interaction effects. How could *this* allocation be performed without the identical problems discussed in Chapter Three emerging in new guise?

The conclusion must be that if we are going to use the capital-budgeting approach to the contributions allocation, we must confine ourselves to saying that *total* firm productivity, the *total* entity situation, has been improved by the decision to buy the new asset. Both for theoretical and for practical reasons, we are not entitled to decompose this total.

Accordingly, the capital-budgeting approach leaves us faced with the following situation. The purchase decision leads to an eventual cash outflow—the cost of obtaining the improvement in the total entity situation. We presently label the related debit figure with the name of the particular kind of new asset acquired. But the decision was made in terms of obtaining the improvement in *total* productivity, and involves changes in the net income effects of all *other* economic goods, too. Vatter's description of this inherent jointness of all inputs is well worth quoting, despite its length:

The joint nature of services is evident even at the point of their acquisition. The process of production is an assimilation of various kinds of services into new combinations; the operations of trading as well as manufacturing businesses are but conversions of services acquired from one set of exchanges into new forms represented by tangible or intangible products that are again exchanged or devoted to final ends. The services thus brought together are not merely contributory to the product; they are also *complementary* to each other. Services are often required because other services have already been acquired; one item frequently trails others along with it, either concomitantly or in sequence. There is no point in hiring workers unless tools and materials are available; unless sheltered working space (heated, lighted, and ventilated), power supply, storerooms, inspection and maintenance crews and facilities, and supervisory and administrative staff are also provided. The combination of resources inherent to carrying on those operations for which a fund of assets is created has the effect of making service capacities joint at the initial stage of acquisition.

---

[10] Diran Bodenhorn, "An Economist Looks at Industrial Accounting and Depreciation," *Accounting Review* XXXVI (October, 1961), 586. *Some* kind of financial statement recognition, either balance sheet or income statement, would be required if the interaction effects are to be given explicit recognition.

Then too, the amount and the kind of service required in the form of one factor of production are affected by alterations in the service available from or required of another—stemming from variations in quality, efficiency, or other variables in the composite picture. The labor required for a given operation may be increased or decreased by alterations in the quality or the specifications of materials; by differences in machine setup or speed; by shifts in the policy or in the efficiency of operations with respect to maintenance; by changes in the intensiveness of inspection, or variations in the degree of quality to be maintained; and, also, by differences in the intelligence and alertness of supervisors, administrators, and workers in their various capacities. Services are jointly related in that there are a number of closely interwoven patterns that exist between them, and these may have different effects under varying conditions.[11]

What we call "the cost of machine so-and-so" is really the cost of getting from one total entity situation to another total entity situation. Perhaps we should instead caption the debit figure "cost of estimated improvement in the firms' total situation achieved on such-and-such a date through a project involving acquisition of machine so-and-so." If nonmonetary asset acquisitions affect all inputs (including many kinds of economic goods that are not even reported as assets), how meaningful is it to classify nonmonetary assets on the balance sheet by individual *kinds of assets?* Doing so involves allocation of the various total productivity improvements to individual inputs. Yet allocation to just one input is even more radically arbitrary than is an allocation which looks only to the separate effects of the various contributing inputs. Perhaps it would make more sense instead to arrange the balance sheet by unexpired costs of projects intended to enhance total entity profitability, arranged by starting date and project purpose.[12]

But even this is hard to defend. Under the capital-budgeting approach, the individual projects, in effect, all blur into each other—or, rather, into the total entity situation that each attempts to improve.[13] The reader should notice that this blurring also occurs under the form of the net-revenue contributions approach discussed in Chapter Three (or, say, were one to approximate the effects of an individual asset by a simulation model). The reasons are the same; in fact, what we are seeing here is that the same basic interaction problem afflicts both the simultaneous-allocation and capital-budgeting forms of the net-revenue contributions approach.

Other interaction effects

The capital-budgeting approach suffers from other interaction problems besides the ones already specifically mentioned. The previous problem arose in part because the approach requires that one speak of the individual net-revenue contributions of an asset as distinct from those of any other inputs. Yet it should be obvious that the notion of such "individual" contributions is a severe abstraction. All economic activity takes place in a *context* of a market, with particular buyers and sellers. The

---

[11] William J. Vatter, *The Fund Theory of Accounting and Its Implications for Financial Reports* (Chicago: University of Chicago Press, 1947), p. 23.

[12] This seems to be what Coughlin was recommending—see John Coughlin, "Industrial Accounting," *Accounting Review*, XXXIV (July, 1959), 427.

[13] One *could* disentangle the factors by calculating how much the product would *decrease* if one factor were removed. But then one would run into the kinds of problems discussed in the next subsection: which one you remove first is an arbitrary decision that affects the calculation, and some factors are not divisible (removal of a conveyor belt may halt production completely).

net-revenue contributions of a lathe in the United States will be different from those of the same lathe in Borneo. For accounting purposes, interactions with this *general* context can be taken for granted (ignored) since the accountant is not responsible for reporting on the activities of other entities. But another part of this context is the firm's other inputs—and these cannot be ignored, since the accountant *is* charged with reporting on *them*.

Similarly, in the capital-budgeting approach we are assuming some previous state. The incremental contribution of the Q-machines is $38 if one is given the previous state, that is, the number of P-machines previously in operation. The amount that any one new input will add to production (and thus its net-revenue contributions) depends on the number and kind of previous inputs. This means that the depreciation pattern depends on the *sequence* of purchases—on all interacting prior inputs. In the previous example of the P-machines and the Q-machines, $84 was allocated to the annual net-revenue contributions of the P-machines and $38 to the annual contributions of the Q-machines. But had the Q-machines been the ones that were available first, the allocation would have been $120 to the P-machines and $2 to the Q-machines![14] Once again the inputs blur. Once again it is artificial to speak of the contributions of the individual input viewed in isolation—to assign any meaning to the notion of separate assets (or to separate expenses, for that matter).

The calculation of net-revenue contributions can easily become entirely arbitrary. An automobile will not run at all without a distributor. If the distributor is the last part added, should the entire contribution of the automobile be allocated to it? Why should the contributions allocation depend on a particular irrelevant order of assembly or sequence of asset acquisitions?[15]

All of this relates to a more general principle, familiar in capital budgeting, that interrelated decisions should be aggregated—should not be made independently of each other:

---

[14] Once again, the basic revenue function is:

$$Z = 20P - P^2 + 3PQ + 13Q - 6Q^2$$

At $P=0$, $Q=2$, this becomes:

$$Z^0 = 0 + 0 + 0 + 26 - 24 = 2$$

Once the six P-machines are acquired, Z' becomes, as before, $122. The net-revenue contributions of the P-machines are therefore:

$$Z' - Z^0 = \$122 - \$2 = \$120.$$

The reader should be aware of another paradox here. Suppose that Q-machines had 4-year service lives and were acquired at the *same time* as the P-machines. Depending on whether one determined a depreciation pattern for the P-machines or the Q-machines first, the investment in the Q-machines would have an average implicit rate of return that was either over 42 percent, or negative!

[15] The same point is made by Devine:

"The expected services for a particular unit depend on a somewhat arbitrary ordering of the unit with regard to the margin. That is, the value of a particular asset depends on its supporting assets and also on its ordering in the acquisition series."

—Carl Thomas Devine, *Essays in Accounting Theory* (privately printed, 1962), II, 260. See also Carl Thomas Devine, "Asset Cost and Expiration," in Morton Backer, editor, *Modern Accounting Theory* (Englewood Cliffs, New Jersey: Prentice-Hall, Inc., 1966), p. 144.

In general, where the costs of one plan affect the costs of another, or the revenues are related, or the costs of one plan affect the revenues of another, we have linked problems; it is necessary to include all the interrelated plans together in one plan, for the same reason that joint products must be considered together. The attempt to isolate one of a group of interrelated plans fails because it attempts to ignore the interrelation which is a condition of the problem. The effect of the plan on the value of the aggregate assets will be calculated wrongly . . .[16]

A major problem with the capital-budgeting approach is that at the level of aggregation faced by the financial accountant, there is considerable interrelation among inputs and therefore a serious danger of interdependence of capital-budgeting decisions.

Why not combine inputs?

This being so, why not avoid the problems of interaction and blurring by *combining* inputs? Published financial statements do not report separate figures for each depreciable asset. Instead, they usually report a single depreciation figure on the income statement and a very few figures for different kinds of depreciable assets on the balance sheet. Why not simply combine figures on the financial statements until the point is reached that a simple additive income function is achieved? For instance, instead of reporting separate *P*-machines and *Q*-machines, why not report *P*–*Q* centers instead, and depreciate on a per center instead of a per machine basis?

The question to be asked is: how pervasive are interaction effects? It is hard to imagine many nonmonetary inputs, other than incidental holdings of securities, that would have the same net-revenue contributions were they divested of the firm. Therefore, it is hard to see how combining could stop much short of a single nonmonetary economic goods center (or perhaps even a single economic goods center including cash and receivables) with a correspondingly radical compression of expense data on the income statement.

In Chapter Six, several possible responses to the financial accountant's allocation problems are discussed. One possibility mentioned is to carry out just such a radical compression of reported financial statement data: in effect to reflect all unexpired nonmonetary goods by a single asset figure on the balance sheet, all nonmonetary goods expirations by a single expense figure on the income statement. It is argued (though the idea does not seem very promising) that this might be appropriate, under one possible model of what investors should want to learn from financial statements. But such compression certainly involves a grave departure from what accountants are presently doing. As we saw in Chapter Three, as contrasted with economists' approaches to the firm, accountants presently provide relatively detailed information about nonmonetary goods. How far can such detailed disclosure be sacrificed and accounting still perform its unique functions?

Reinvestment

The individual projects blur into one another for an additional reason. Table 4–2 depicts two projects, both of which cost $1,100 at the beginning of Year 1.

---

[16] J. R. Gould, "The Economist's Cost Concept and Business Problems," in W. T. Baxter and Sidney Davidson, editors, *Studies in Accounting Theory* (Homewood, Illinois: Richard D. Irwin, Inc., 1962), pp. 232–33.

TABLE 4-2

Two Investments, Each with a 10% Average Rate of Return

	Estimated Net-Revenue Contributions		
	Year 1	Year 2	Year 3
Project *A*..............	$510.00	$470.00	$ 330.00
Project *B*.............	-0-	-0-	1,464.10

The capital-budgeting approach regards both of these projects as having the same (10 percent) average rate of return. But for Project *A* to leave the firm as well off at the end of Year 3 as Project *B*, its proceeds must be reinvested at 10 percent. Project *A*'s net-revenue contributions themselves add up to only $1,310.00 (510+470 +330=1,310). Reinvestment at 10 percent is required to make the two projects equivalent:

$$\$510.00\times1.10\times1.10.....................\$ 617.10$$
$$\$470.00\times1.10..........................\ 517.00$$
$$\$330.00 ....\ 330.00$$

$$\text{Total} ....\$1,464.10$$

This example demonstrates that the capital-budgeting approach assumes reinvestment at the same rate of return as the project rate.[17] But this can be reversed by saying that unless the reinvestment rate *is* the same as the project rate, the expectations from one project cannot be considered independently from the expectations of subsequent projects—and that, in general, successive projects cannot be considered independently of each other. Instead, one is confronted with an endless branching series of future contributions that rapidly become intertwined with other endless branching series. As Brown remarks:

. . . cash flows available for reinvestment at any particular time are typically derived from numerous projects and constitute a homogeneous pool of capital at management's disposal; identification of specific segments of this pool with individual reinvestment proposals is possible on only an arbitrary basis.[18]

Since the capital-budgeting approach treats all projects as occurring in sequence, once again the individual projects tend to blur into one another.[19]

[17] See William J. Vatter, "Income Models, Book Yield, and the Rate of Return," *Accounting Review*, XLI (October, 1966), 690–92 for a different presentation of the same point. See also Victor H. Brown, "Rate of Return: Some Comments on Its Applicability in Capital Budgeting," *Accounting Review*, XXXVI (January, 1961), 52–53. The capital-budgeting approach must make *some* kind of assumption, implicit or explicit, about reinvestment, since it is based in a technique intended for comparing alternative projects.

Since I am making frequent use of Vatter's analysis in this study, it should be noted that we reach opposed conclusions about depreciation. Vatter tries to show that a particular approach to depreciation is justifiable. I agree that his approach is as well-justified as any, but do not believe that it can be conclusively defended against all alternatives—the arguments are presented in the next chapter.

[18] Brown (1961), p. 53.

[19] Maintenance offers a similar example of input interaction: the lives of most depreciable assets may be extended if additional inputs of materials, labor, and so forth are provided by way of maintenance.

Significance of the income statement

All of this demonstrates that the capital-budgeting approach leads to a very different interpretation of the balance sheet than that which we usually give to it—one with which few of us would be comfortable, one which seems ultimately to lead to reporting all nonmonetary inputs by a single figure. But perhaps this is bearable: some accountants have argued that effects on balance sheets are not very important.[20]

However, the significance of the depreciation figures on the *income statement* also becomes different from that which we would like to give them. The following remarks of the AAA's Committee on The Matching Concept reflect the kind of interpretation that most of us would like to give to depreciation expense:

In business operations, costs, defined as resources given up or economic sacrifices made, are incurred with the anticipation that they will produce revenue in excess of the outlay. Within this frame of reference, one can then say that costs constitute one measure of business effort, and revenues represent accomplishments coming from those efforts. Appropriate reporting of costs and revenues should therefore relate costs with revenues in such a way as to disclose most vividly the relationships between efforts and accomplishments.[21]

The capital-budgeting approach does not lead to comparing current accomplishments with the efforts necessary to achieve them. Instead, it leads to comparing current accomplishments (*actual* revenues or cost savings) with amounts determined by the figures used in the contributions allocation. And these latter figures depend on expectations held in the *past* (at the time that the asset was purchased) of what current accomplishments would be. These past expectations and the current performance will not be the same (except by coincidence) if any new interacting inputs have been acquired meanwhile. And, as we have seen, the expectations associated with the old assets cannot be changed to reflect the acquisition of the new inputs.

Therefore, in effect the capital-budgeting approach leads to comparing actual accomplishments with a variety of obsolete estimates of what the efforts *might* have *been* to achieve some *other* set of accomplishments.[22] This is not a satisfactory com-

---

[20] For example, see Eldon S. Hendriksen, *Accounting Theory* (Homewood, Illinois: Richard D. Irwin, Inc., 1965), p. 306.

[21] 1964 Concepts and Standards Research Study Committee—The Matching Concept, "The Matching Concept," *Accounting Review*, XL (April, 1965), 368. See also Rufus Wixon and Walter G. Kell, editors, *Accountants' Handbook* (New York: The Ronald Press Company, 1960), p. (1–17).

[22] Essentially the same point was made by Canning—see Canning (1929), p. 231. Compare Arnett's recent comments (made in a different context):

"Economists are generally concerned with the allocation of resources among competing uses. Expectations are of prime importance in this regard. Accountants are concerned with accurately reflecting what has happened . . . management's plans (budgeting for example) reflect its expectations, but data reflected on a historical basis reflect the extent to which these expectations have been realized. Such a comparison is important to management for present control and future planning purposes, since only an accurate reflection of past results can be used as a springboard for future expectations. It is also essential information for present and potential owners. These persons wish to know how close to expectations actual results have been."
—Harold E. Arnett, "Importance of Capital Gains and Losses in Investment Analysis," *Financial Analysts Journal*, XXIII (January–February, 1967), 46.

The accountant who uses the capital-budgeting approach is making much the same mistake as the middle-aged man who uses the expectations of the honeymoon to evaluate his wife's present accomplishments as a mother, cook, companion, and so forth. One *stays* married for reasons other than one *gets* married. Similarly, the services provided by the depreciable asset (should it be *possible* to separately identify them) are rarely those anticipated at the time of purchase.

parison. It is even less satisfactory when we recognize (as was indicated by the discussion of the balance sheet) that depreciation reflects the amortization of the costs of an improvement in the total entity situation, and represents the write-off of costs of improved productivity of labor and many other inputs. Just as all nonmonetary economic goods inputs blur into one another on the balance sheet, so the distinctions among different kinds of expenses blur, too. This is what one would expect: after all, the kinds of changes reflected in the income statement *always* will be parallelled by corresponding changes in balance sheet assets and liabilities—the two statements are intimately linked.

Summary

In some cases, it may be possible to estimate the future stream of revenues and costs to the firm and, by discounting appropriately the expected stream of net output values, an estimate of the current valuation of the entire firm may be obtained. But it is not possible to assign this stream of net output values to specific assets. All operating assets contribute to this revenue stream, but it is a joint contribution; there is no way to determine how much each asset contributes . . . .While arbitrary allocation methods could be used, the result would not be meaningful for financial reporting.[23]

Under the capital-budgeting approach, the contributions allocation consists of associating the entire sequence of changes in estimated income with the new asset—despite that this sequence is a joint result of the activities of all entity inputs. The results of this allocation are then used in conducting *another* allocation (the depreciation allocation) whereby the acquisition price of the new asset is allocated to the activities of the various service years. Why? Because (as Chapter Three demonstrated) one cannot do the natural-seeming thing and use the net-revenue contributions of the *component* to determine the allocation of the component.

But this is merely a negative reason. Are there any positive reasons for using the change in the totality in this way? To claim that we should use the capital-budgeting approach because the new asset "caused" the change is to take an arbitrarily narrow view of causation. *All* of the inputs caused the change.

Lacking positive justification, negative justification will suffice only when one may insist that circumstances require that *some* depreciation method must be used (and all other possibilities have been exhausted). But to assert this is circularly to assert the issue under inquiry: Chapter Six will argue that there are several possible approaches that avoid the whole net-revenue-contributions approach (in either its simultaneous-allocation or capital-budgeting forms)—including the approach of not depreciating assets at all.

Besides this, of course, it has been demonstrated that if the capital-budgeting approach is not to be arbitrary, we must usually follow reporting practices that most accountants would reject: reporting all nonmonetary inputs by a single asset figure on the balance sheet and a single expense figure on the income statement. For without being arbitrary it is impossible to distinguish the separate contributions of individual inputs (except through the chaotic expedient of giving explicit recognition to all interaction effects—an approach that leads to similar allocation problems, anyway);[24]

---

[23] Hendriksen (1965), p. 288.

[24] Compare the following:

". . . values are fundamentally to be associated with the state or condition of the entire system, and not necessarily with some linear combinations of the things comprising it."

—Nicolas M. Smith, "A Calculus for Ethics: A Theory of the Structure of Value—Part I," *Behavioral Science*,

in fact, the arguments in this chapter have demonstrated that under the capital-budgeting approach it usually is impossible (without being arbitrary) to distinguish these inputs *themselves* from each other. And this balance sheet problem generates a parallel difficulty in distinguishing different kinds of expenses from each other on the income statement: if the inputs can't be distinguished from each other, neither can their expirations. Everything blurs into everything else.[25]

I (April, 1956), 112, quoted by Richard Mattessich, *Accounting and Analytical Methods* (Homewood, Illinois: Richard D. Irwin, Inc., 1964), p. 206.

[25] The reader should not conclude that the foregoing discussion exhausts the list of difficulties associated with the capital-budgeting approach. Others may be found mentioned in F. K. Wright, "Towards a General Theory of Depreciation," *Journal of Accounting Research*, II (Spring, 1964), 87–90.

Finally, it should be pointed out that the capital-budgeting approach does not necessarily involve depreciating the asset in terms of the particular pattern of net-revenue contributions that led to the decision to acquire the asset! The following example demonstrates this. Suppose that machines A and B are mutually exclusive investments, and that the company is employing the capital-budgeting approach to investment decisions, at a 10% rate of discount. Suppose that the machines both cost $10,000 and offer the following pattern of cash flows:

Machine	End-of-Year Cash Flow			Net Present Value (10%)	Line
	Year 0	Year 1	Year 2		
A........	$(10,000)	$ 4,000	$8,000	$248	1
B........	(10,000)	$ 8,000	3,400	83	2
Difference....	–0–	$(4,900)	$4,600	$165	3

Machine A would be chosen, since it has the larger net present value. But it is chosen because of the cash-flow pattern shown in Line 3 (which compares the decision to buy machine A with the next best alternative decision). The capital-budgeting approach does not use the Line 3 cash flow pattern. Instead, it uses the pattern shown in Line 1, which compares the decision to buy Machine A with the *third* best alternative: making no investment at all.

CHAPTER FIVE

The Depreciation Allocation: Problems
of Allocation Over Time

UNDER the net-revenue-contributions approach, once the contributions allocation has determined the asset's net-revenue contributions during its years of service life, these contributions are used to determine the asset's depreciation pattern. As was indicated in Chapter Three (see pp. 36–37), the pattern is determined as follows.

First, it is assumed that the same average implicit rate of return, r_j, applies in all years. This rate of return is calculated as that number such that:

$$K_j = \sum_{t=1}^{N} \frac{Y_j(t)}{(1 + r_j)^t}$$

where K_j represents the asset's acquisition price, $Y_j(t)$ is its net-revenue contribution in Year t, and the asset's service life is estimated to be N years. The depreciation allocated to any year is the difference between the asset's book value at the beginning and end of the year, where the book value at the time of acquisition equals the acquisition price, and thereafter equals the following at the end of any year, h ($h=1, \cdots, N$):

$$\sum_{t=h+1}^{N} \frac{Y_j(t)}{(1 + r_j)^{t-h}}$$

This final depreciation allocation is the subject of this chapter.

I. Interaction Over Time

The various difficulties of the contributions allocation (discussed in the previous two chapters) result mainly from the presence of interaction effects. These contributions allocations were allocations among different kinds of inputs. The depreciation allocation is an allocation *among different years*. However, similar interaction effects exist among years and lead to much the same kinds of problems of jointness that we have faced before.[1] In the last chapter we already saw one aspect of this problem when we discussed changes in estimates, and another when we discussed the reinvestment problem. Here is another.[2]

Ambiguities in rates of return

The net-revenue-contributions approach assumes that the same implicit rate of

---

[1] Writing about similar relationships, Cohen observes:

"A simulation model which purports to portray evolutionary behavior over many successive time periods involves a very high order of joint determination of all the endogenous variables, stretching over the entire time span which is simulated."

—Kalman J. Cohen, "Simulation of the Firm," *American Economic Review*, L (May, 1960), 539.

[2] The arguments in this section are closely related to those in William J. Vatter, "Income Models, Book Yield, and the Rate of Return," *Accounting Review*, XLI (October, 1966), 684–90. Similar arguments can be found in William J. Vatter, "Accounting for Leases," *Journal of Accounting Research*, IV (Autumn, 1966), 138–42. Compare George J. Staubus, "Decreasing Charge Depreciation—Still Searching for Logic," *Accounting Review*, XXXVII (July, 1962), 497–501. See also Orace Johnson, "Two General Concepts of Depreciation," *Journal of Accounting Research*, VI (Spring, 1968), 32–37; Johnson describes the basic ambiguity discussed here, though from a different vantage point. Finally, see the related discussion in Gabriel A. D. Preinreich, "Annual Survey of Economic Theory: The Theory of Depreciation," *Econometrica*, VI (July, 1938), 236–39.

return applies in all years of the asset's service life. Now, it is proper to speak of the average implicit rate of return on the investment in a depreciable asset *over the life of the project as a whole*. But within any one year that implicit rate of return is ambiguous. So, therefore, is the related depreciation allocation.

This can be made clear by referring back to Table 2–2 (page 20)—wherein depreciation was calculated by the net-revenue-contributions approach for an investment with a 10 percent average rate of return. As was emphasized, in Table 2–2 it is assumed that 10 percent is not only the *average* rate of return over the three-year project, but also that the rate of return *in each year* is 10 percent. Yet there are any number of other sequences of within-year rates of return that might be assumed instead, and which would be consistent with an average rate of 10 percent over the project as a whole. Table 5–1 gives one such set of annual rates of return.[3] Notice that the resulting depreciation pattern differs from that in Table 2-2. Table 5-2 gives some additional examples, all of them calculated in the same way as Table 5-1.[4] Many

TABLE 5-1

CALCULATION OF ANNUAL DEPRECIATION FOR AN INVESTMENT WITH A 10% AVERAGE RATE OF RETURN
(A DIFFERENT RATE OF RETURN CHOSEN FOR EACH YEAR)

Year	(A) Current Year Rate of Return	(B) Investment (Beginning-of-Year Book Value)	(C) Appropriate Earnings for Year ($A \times B$)	(D) Estimated Net-Revenue Contributions	Depreciation for the Year ($D-C$)
1.........	5.000%	$1,100	$55	$510	$ 455
2.........	13.473%	645	87	470	383
3.........	26.000%	262	68	330	262
Total..					$1,100

[3] The rates for the first and third years were chosen in an arbitrary way—my wife's birthday is on May 26 (5/26). The Year 2 rate was chosen to generate a 10 percent average rate of return. The algebra here is very simple. We already know that for a $1,100 investment the following net-revenue contributions will give a 10 percent average implicit rate of return:

Year 1....................$510
Year 2....................470
Year 3....................330

Let r_1, r_2, and r_3 be the rates of return in Years 1, 2, and 3. The only constraints on the r's are that:

$$\frac{510}{(1+r_1)} + \frac{470}{(1+r_1)(1+r_2)} + \frac{330}{(1+r_1)(1+r_2)(1+r_3)} = 1,100$$

Given that $r_1=0.05$ and $r_3=0.26$, we can solve for $r_2=0.13473$.

[4] The final column to the right in Table 5-2 represents the interesting case wherein the accountant depreciates the asset in terms of the *relative* net-revenue contributions in each year, without worrying about rates of return: $510+$470+$330=$1,310.

Year	Annual Depreciation
1.........$1,100×(510/1,310) =	$ 428
2.........$1,100×(470/1,310) =	395
3.........$1,100×(330/1,310) =	277
	$1,100

TABLE 5-2

ANNUAL DEPRECIATION FOR AN INVESTMENT WITH A 10% AVERAGE RATE OF RETURN UNDER
DIFFERENT ASSUMPTIONS AS TO THE RATE OF RETURN CHOSEN FOR EACH YEAR

Depreciation for the Year	Pattern of Current-Year Rates of Return						
	18.000%	10.000%	9.732%	5.000%	0.500%	7.455%	Year 1
	1.000% •	10.000%	5.000%	13.473%	20.000%	11.161%	Year 2
	1.264%	10.000%	26.000%	26.000%	34.955%	19.133%	Year 3
Year 1......	$ 312	$ 400	$ 403	$ 455	$ 504	$ 428	
Year 2......	462	400	435	383	351	395	
Year 3......	326	300	262	262	245	277	
Total.....	$1,100	$1,100	$1,100	$1,100	$1,100	$1,100	

other patterns are also possible. Without employing any negative within-year rates of return, Year 1 depreciation could be anywhere between $300 and $510—the range of ambiguity is about 25 percent on either side of the constant-rate-of-return figures. Depreciation in Year 3 could be anywhere between $330 and $120—from 110 percent to 40 percent of the constant-rate-of-return figure.[5]

The point that should be emphasized here is that the particular pattern of annual implicit rates of return chosen represents a *decision*—whether that pattern be 18%-1%-1.264%, 5%-13.473%-26%, or 10%-10%-10%. This conclusion parallels one discussed in Chapter Two, in which it was demonstrated that the choice of conventional straight-line depreciation also represents a decision. The argument here is essentially the same as it was there.[6] The net-revenue-contributions approach re-

Even in this case the average rate of return over the whole project is still 10 percent, and we still can specify the implicit rate of return assumed in each year. Any depreciation pattern chosen has *some* pattern of annual rates of return implicit in it; there is no way to avoid making some assumption about within-year rates of return. In this case the assumption really is one of equal cost per dollar of net-revenue contributions. For theoretical justification, such an assumption must be defended, and its defense would be made especially difficult by the likelihood of market imperfections: equal cost per dollar of net-revenue contributions is apt to be only an ideal, or a simplifying assumption.

Year	(W) Depreciation for the Year	(X) Estimated Net-Revenue Contributions	(Y) Appropriate Earnings for Year $(X-W)$	(Z) Investment (Beginning-of-Year Book Value)	Current Year Rate of Return $(Y \div Z)$
1..........	$428	$510	$82	$1,100	7.455%
2..........	395	470	75	672	11.161%
3..........	277	330	53	277	19.133%

[5] This range of ambiguity for any one year will be determined by the total profit over the entire service life of the project—here $210 (510+470+330−1,100=210). The reader will recall that it is assumed that no negative rates of return are employed. So, in any *one* year, the earnings may be as low as $0 or as high as the total profit, and the current year rate of return will vary commensurately. The longer-lived the asset and the higher the average rate of return, the greater this total profit and the greater the range of ambiguity will be within any one year. The reader can easily verify that the particular example given here is a relatively mild and understated one.

[6] The argument will not be repeated here, except in summary. It is particularly easy to see the element of choice involved in assuming a uniform rate in all years when one considers investments in assets whose net-revenue contributions do not begin until several years after the investment has been made. Some kinds of assets involved in production of new products fit this description. The situation is common in agriculture. A former

quires that *some* decision be made (explicitly or implicitly) about within-year rates of return. If one's depreciation pattern is to be theoretically justified, that decision must be defended against all competing approaches. But how is this to be done here? There seems little (either in rules with which laymen would agree or in economic theory) to which a conclusive appeal might be made.[7] Evidently, any decision made, and therefore any resulting depreciation pattern, must be arbitrary. The trouble here is that the rate-of-return calculus is not concerned with the results within individual years at all, but only with the results of the whole project.[8] Therefore, one ends up faced with a kind of indivisible jointness of annual rates of return that is very similar to the jointness that has faced us elsewhere in this study.[9]

Other Difficulties

The foregoing do not exhaust the difficulties that haunt the net-revenue-contributions approach. Brown mentions another situation, fortunately quite rare: occasionally investments have an infinite rate of return. Brown's example is of a firm purchasing an existing business with annual net cash flows of $20,000 for $100,000:

---

colleague provides an exotic example: cocoa trees take ten to fifteen years to mature; their production decreases to practically nothing after their twentieth year. Almost all net-revenue contributions are received in the last five of the asset's 20-year life—Paul Frishkoff, "The Dilemma of West African Commerce, 1899–1955" (unpublished), p. 15. While it is perfectly possible to assume a uniform rate of return on such an investment, it is obvious that an assumption *has* been made.

The reader should also consider Gellein's arguments for an increasing rate of discount for successive estimated net-revenue contributions—see Oscar S. Gellein, "The Decreasing-Charge Concept," *Journal of Accountancy*, C (August, 1955), 58–59.

[7] Appendix A of this chapter looks at one direction to which an appeal might be made: the certainty equivalents approach. However, the appeal runs into the same kinds of difficulties as do other approaches examined. A possible appeal to laymen is examined in the next chapter.

[8] The approach to depreciation suggested by Lowe leads to similar problems—see Howard D. Lowe, "The Essentials of a General Theory of Depreciation," *Accounting Review*, XXXVIII (April, 1963), 293–301. Lowe considers the total annual cost of operating a plant to be the sum of a "capital charge" (the sum of depreciation and implicit interest on the investment), and a "current cost" (comprising all other expenditures) (p. 294). The key assumption under his system (p. 294) is that total cost *in every year* should be reported as no greater than the cost of the most economical alternative to providing the related services in this way. Then, a deductive argument is presented that (given certain additional economic assumptions) the depreciation pattern of the plant is determined (pp. 294–97).

However, once the entity has committed itself to an investment in plant, it has thereby lost much of its original freedom to choose among economic alternatives. There is no reason to believe that total cost in every year *will* be no greater than the total cost of the best alternative. All one is entitled to assume is that current cost will not persistently exceed the total cost of the best alternative. Furthermore, notice that even when the initial decision to buy the plant was made, it was possible that in some years an alternative investment was preferable—so long as the present value calculation revealed an *over-all* superiority for the investment actually made.

[9] Compare the ambiguity discussed in F. K. Wright, "Towards a General Theory of Depreciation," *Journal of Accounting Research*, II (Spring, 1964), 84–85. Wright's suggested way to resolve this ambiguity requires that depreciation figures be consistent with a particular idealized economic model—one which is as hard to defend conclusively as is the idealized notion of identical rates of return in each year (Wright's approach is not discussed in detail here because it is examined from another vantage point in the next chapter).

Another implicit use of an idealized economic model is found in Stephen H. Sosnick, "Depreciation: The Offsetting-Interest Method," *Accounting Review*, XXXVII (January, 1962), 59–66. Sosnick points out that in the interval between purchase and replacement of a fixed asset cash inflows are being generated that exceed cash outflows. The excess ordinarily will be reinvested, and there will be a resulting tendency for income to rise throughout the interval, then fall abruptly after the reinvestment. Sosnick's offsetting-interest method is designed to eliminate this effect and insure that reported net earnings will have no tendency to change over the life of the asset. But once again the criterion of equal reported net income in each year is not defended. (As Wright points out—see Wright [1964], p. 87—Sosnick's method also assumes that it is possible to identify specific revenues or cash flows with individual depreciable assets—an assumption which the arguments developed since Chapter Two render illegitimate.)

for personal tax reasons the previous owner wishes to be paid nothing initially, then $10,000 annually for 10 years.[10] Similarly, Bierman and Smidt discuss investments for which there is *no* rate of return.[11]

The following problem also has received attention in the literature. Refer again to our original example of the net-revenue-contributions approach, Table 2-2 (page 20). This table could have been presented in a different manner. At the time the asset was purchased, the present values of the annual net-revenue contributions were as shown in Table 5-3. Assuming that the original estimates were correct, Table 5-4 shows the

TABLE 5-3

PRESENT VALUES OF NET-REVENUE CONTRIBUTIONS AT BEGINNING OF YEAR 1

Year of Receipt	(A) Net-Revenue Contributions	Number of Years Until Net-Revenue Contributions Are Received	(B) Appropriate Discount Factor (at 10%)	Present Value (A × B)
1.............	$510	1	0.9091	$ 464
2.............	470	2	0.8264	388
3.............	330	3	0.7513	248
Present value, beginning of Year 1..				$1,100

TABLE 5-4

PRESENT VALUES OF NET-REVENUE CONTRIBUTIONS AT END OF YEAR 1

Year of Receipt	(A) Net-Revenue Contributions	Number of Years Until Net-Revenue Contributions Are Received	(B) Appropriate Discount Factor (at 10%)	Present Value (A × B)
2.............	$470	1	0.9091	$427
3.............	330	2	0.8264	273
Present value, end of Year 1...				$700

situation after one year has passed. Therefore, the $400 of depreciation allocated to Year 1 could be interpreted as follows:

Present value, beginning of Year 1..................	$1,100
Present value, end of Year 1.......................	700
Depreciation for Year 1..........................	$ 400

This agrees with the description of the net-revenue-contributions approach given at the start of Chapter Three.

But this is not the only way that one could do things. One could instead perceive the purchaser of the machine as having acquired three years' net-revenue contri-

---

[10] Victor H. Brown, "Rate of Return: Some Comments on Its Applicability in Capital Budgeting," *Accounting Review*, XXXVI (January, 1961), 57–58—the example could be modified to allow interest to the seller.

[11] Harold Bierman, Jr., and Seymour Smidt, *The Capital Budgeting Decision*, Second Edition (New York: The Macmillan Company, 1966) p. 47.

butions, the first of which cost $464, the second $388, and the third $248—and argue that the appropriate depreciation for Year 1 should be $464, and so forth. This is the "Revco" depreciation approach suggested by Dixon.[12] Nor is this the only possible alternative. By obtaining services from the asset in Year 1, the company has forgone services that it might otherwise have received, perhaps, in Years 3 and 4. Suppose that by receiving $510 of net-revenue contributions in Year 1, the firm sacrificed $110 of contributions that would otherwise have been received in Year 3 and $400 that otherwise would have been received in Year 4. The beginning-of-Year-1 present value (10 percent) of these sacrifices is approximately $356 . . . this particular approach gets a bit complicated, but it *has* been suggested in the literature under a different guise.[13]

Summary

Chapters Three and Four discussed the difficulties that input interactions cause for the contributions analysis, perceiving this problem as one of allocations made *within* individual years. But the net-revenue-contributions approach involves *two* allocations. The second (the depreciation allocation) allocates *among* years. As the previous examples (of which the first is the most important) indicate, the depreciation allocation suffers from much the same problems of jointness, interaction effects, and ambiguity as does the contributions allocation.

So far, our discussion has concerned conventional approaches to depreciation. We concluded in Chapter Two that conventional depreciation methods must either use a net-revenue contributions approach or else be arbitrary. But the discussion *since* Chapter Two has demonstrated that for the net-revenue-contributions approach to avoid being arbitrary itself, interaction effects must be absent. Moreover, this absence of interaction effects must hold true when the revenue function is viewed over time, as well as within individual years. Otherwise, the net-revenue-contributions approach leads to grave ambiguities that are insoluble under present allocation theory within the framework of conventional accounting. *Unless interaction effects are absent, both within and among years, the net-revenue-contributions approach will give arbitrary results.* And it is clear that interaction effects usually will be present.

Of course there may be a few instances in which this will not be true. There may be cases in which net-revenue contributions can be isolated with respect to specific assets or groups of assets, and where there is no interaction over time. The example of individual securities in a portfolio has been suggested (but the reader should see Appendix B to this chapter, which suggests that ambiguities exist over time even with securities).

With regard to expenses, it might be argued that there are cases in which *exact* allocation is impossible, but where one still may wish to employ the net-revenue-contributions approach to determine an *approximate* depreciation pattern. For example, the sequence of maintenance, labor, and fuel costs for one machine may have a significantly different time shape from that for another machine, even though both machines operate jointly to produce the same revenue; in such cases

---

[12] See Robert L. Dixon, "Decreasing Charge Depreciation—A Search for Logic," *Accounting Review*, XXXV (October, 1960), 590–97; Arthur N. Lorig, "On the Logic of Decreasing Charge Depreciation," *Accounting Review*, XXXVII (January, 1962), 56–58; and Staubus (1962).

[13] See Myron H. Ross, "Depreciation and User Cost," *Accounting Review*, XXXV (July, 1960), 424.

differing depreciation patterns for the two machines might be urged. However, the arguments since Chapter Two indicate that at best only a *partial* defense would be possible here; so the choice of depreciation patterns still would be arbitrary. (It should be emphasized again that just as financial accounting presently lacks a systematic theory for behavior in the face of ignorance, so it presently lacks any theoretically justified way of ranking arbitrariness, of saying "this method is less arbitrary than that," or "this kind of arbitrariness is preferable to that kind," and to defend one's choice conclusively.)

Even the extent to which partial defenses are possible will depend in part on just how serious the "blurring" together of nonmonetary economic goods really is. How far is it possible to distinguish individual inputs once they have joined the common input pool? The answer depends on the *extent* of interaction effects at the level of aggregation employed by accountants, another matter where research would be highly valuable. However, it should be emphasized that the last two chapters have provided *prima-facie* evidence that these interaction effects are so extensive that such partial defenses are not apt to be feasible—except by ignoring what may be the most important aspects of the situation.

Pending possible future research, we should admit that the net-revenue-contributions approach usually will be arbitrary. The problems discussed since Chapter Two seem serious and pervasive enough that it is fair to place the burden of proof on those who wish to employ this approach to demonstrate that the particular facts of the situation justify its use. Since we saw in Chapter Two that all *other* conventional depreciation approaches were arbitrary, we may conclude that all conventional depreciation methods should be regarded as giving arbitrary results unless those who wish to employ them can prove otherwise.[14]

II. THE OVER-ALL ALLOCATION PROBLEM

At the beginning of this study it was asserted that although depreciable assets would be used as an example, the allocation problems to be discussed pertained to all nonmonetary economic goods (including many that never are reported as assets in published financial statements). By now the reason for this assertion should be obvious. In most cases examined, the allocation problems discussed in previous chapters have been ones of inability to distinguish depreciable assets (or their depreciation, or their net-revenue contributions) from other economic goods (or *their* write-offs, or net-revenue contributions), or of interactions among depreciable assets and such goods.

And these other economic goods have not just been other depreciable assets. They have been *all* entity inputs. The conclusion reached in the last three chapters is that when the entity's revenue function incorporates interaction effects, the net-revenue-contributions approach usually will find *all* nonmonetary inputs hopelessly entangled,

---

[14] *The reader should notice that this whole critique has been conducted without reference to the usual criticisms of depreciation approaches*: that they are subjective or that they demand estimates which are difficult to make because of the uncertainties of the future. The latter objection certainly is *also* a valid criticism of the net-revenue-contributions approach in practice. But "subjectivity and uncertainty in the estimates" cannot explain why the depreciation problem has not yet been solved on the *theoretical* level. Of course, it is agreed that these estimates are made *additionally* difficult by the very sorts of things discussed in this study. Subjectivity and uncertainty are not the only problems with these estimates—the estimates themselves are affected by the interactions and inherent ambiguities that have been described since Chapter Two.

blurred together. Maximum blurring will occur with goods that have undergone transformation within the firm. For example, the cost of manufactured goods sold is an allocation of finished goods cost. Finished goods costs in turn result from allocations of many other inputs (some of which may involve additional intermediate allocations). But the point to be stressed is that severe blurring may be expected even when such transformations are not involved.

The other nonmonetary economic goods are in the same boat as the depreciable assets. The same arguments can be advanced that:

1. Conventional accounting employs three approaches to treatment of these goods: arbitrary, net-revenue-contributions, and other-services.

2. The other-services approach cannot be applied independently, but only as either an arbitrary or a net-revenue-contributions approach.

3. For almost all goods, the net-revenue-contributions approach must be arbitrary, too.

This means, for example, that the allocation problems discussed are as much at the heart of the accountant's inventory problems as of his depreciation problems.[15] And just as there presently can be no general theoretical solution to the depreciation problem (within the framework of present allocation theory and conventional accounting rules), so there can be no general theoretical solution to the inventory problem within its present framework; present inventory allocations are arbitrary, too. The same is true of allocations of other nonmonetary inputs. In Chapter One it was observed that the accountant's allocation problems with nonmonetary economic goods overlap (and form a major part of) his problems of cost-accumulation and matching. With this in mind, the conclusions may be generalized as follows:

Insofar as cost-accumulation and matching involve allocations of nonmonetary economic goods, these allocations presently are almost always arbitrary; no general solution to this problem is possible within the framework of present allocation theory and present conventional rules.

This conclusion should not surprise us. During the past 75 years or so some extremely good minds have been searching, without success, for such a general solution. But the arguments developed in the previous chapters *do* help explain why no such general solution has been discovered.

III. A Few Empirical Difficulties

A point has been made of ignoring empirical difficulties (such as those involved in estimation) so as to be able to concentrate on more fundamental problems. But a few words about related empirical difficulties would be a suitable conclusion to the discussion of conventional accounting's allocations.

Actual revenue functions must be estimated from time series data. There are a number of implicit conditions which these estimates must satisfy if the figures are to be theoretically justified.[16] When these conditions are *not* satisfied, there will be am-

---

[15] See, for example, William J. Vatter, *The Fund Theory of Accounting and Its Implications for Financial Reports* (Chicago: The University of Chicago Press, 1947), p. 104.

[16] There is a good discussion of these conditions in Robert E. Jensen, "A Multiple Regression Model for Cost Control—Assumptions and Limitations," *Accounting Review*, XLII (April, 1967), 265–73. See also George J. Benston, "Multiple Regression Analysis of Cost Behavior," *Accounting Review*, XLI (October, 1966), 657–72; and John S. Chiu and Don T. DeCoster, "Multiple Product Costing by Multiple Correlation Analysis," *Accounting Review*, XLI (October, 1966), 678–79.

biguities similar to those discussed earlier. For example, one of the difficulties with Cobb-Douglas functions is that there can be a serious problem of multicollinearity among inputs (the variables are correlated with each other, they change in the same ways). When this occurs, it is difficult to identify the separate effects of individual inputs. In theory this problem can be alleviated by obtaining more data. But, for the individual firm, obtaining more data often requires extending the time series further and further backward—and that *also* leads to invalid results if there have been significant changes in the firm's revenue function over time. It also leads to problems of data availability. Besides, the further back one extends the time series, the greater the standard error of the related regression forecast; and the more individual inputs to be estimated, the greater will be the number of period observations required to maintain the necessary degrees of freedom. While these are not difficulties in "pure" allocation theory, such estimation problems are part of any *operational* theory.

Dynamics

So far, this study has discussed interactions among inputs within a single year, and interactions of the depreciation allocations of the single asset over time. But there is a third possibility: interactions among different inputs over time. Relationships over time may have much the same jointness as those within any one year. Actual production, revenue, and income functions will usually be dynamic.[17] They will change over time as the firm becomes more familiar with making and selling its old products, and as it introduces new products (the learning curve reflects one of several reasons for this). They also will be dynamic in the sense that the company's input composition and output mix change gradually over time in lagged response to comparisons of actual results with expectations, to changes in exogenous factors, and so forth.

Incorporation of dynamics in the production, revenue, and income functions tends to require incorporation of among-year interaction effects. For example, consider the variable direct cost associated with running a machine in a particular year. This cost will often be made up of two components. First, there will be the costs of running a brand new machine that has just been broken in—that is, the costs of running a machine that is at the peak of its efficiency. In addition, there will be costs of use. The older machine is apt to require more maintenance. It may require more skilled (higher priced) operators, and so forth. To some extent these additional costs will be related to the amount of output that the machine has already produced in prior years.

No attempt is made here to inquire closely into the effects of dynamics upon allocations. It is sufficient if we are aware that in a dynamic situation the various factors are closely interrelated over time. At any point during the period covered by the dynamic relationship, there is just too much input that has yet to complete its full effect on output for one to be confident about giving theoretical justification to input allocations.

---

[17] This is not the *only* reason for jointness over time. Inputs interact over time in other ways too. For example, a change in wage rates may influence decisions to buy machinery. Similarly, the timing of a depreciable asset's retirement is a major factor in determining the pattern of that asset's net-revenue contributions. An extra year of service changes the contributions pattern and the implicit rate of return used in determining the depreciation allocation. Yet the timing of replacements is affected by various considerations related to other present and prospective depreciable assets, and to other inputs generally.

Appendix A

Certainty Equivalents

In Chapter Five it was argued that the particular pattern of annual implicit rates of return chosen represents a decision, and that there seemed no rule to which laymen would agree, nor anything in economic theory to which a conclusive appeal could be made, that would justify choice of one pattern over the unlimited number of other possible patterns. However, one possibility is worth investigation, if only as another example of the kinds of difficulties such attempts at justification encounter: the "certainty equivalents" approach.[18]

Our basic relationship that the implicit annual rates of return must satisfy is:

$$K_j = \sum_{t=1}^{N} \frac{Y_j(t)}{[1 + r_j(t)]^t}$$

Where K_j represents the acquisition price of a depreciable asset, j, N is the estimated service life of asset j in years, $Y_j(t)$ is the estimated net-revenue contributions of asset j in Year t, and $r_j(t)$ is the implicit rate of return on asset j in Year t. According to proponents of the certainty equivalents approach the discounting process *per se* should involve only the time-value of money; adjustments for risk should be handled separately. Therefore, they would substitute the risk-free rate, i (often considered as the rate on U. S. Treasury securities) for $r_j(t)$, and convert the previous relationship into:

$$K_j = \sum_{t=1}^{N} \frac{R_j(t) \cdot Y_j(t)}{(1 + i)^t}$$

where $R_j(t)$ is the certainty equivalent coefficient. $R_j(t)$ will vary between zero and one, inversely with the degree of risk estimated for Year t's net-revenue contributions. The problem of defending a particular pattern of annual rates of return vanishes. Of course, in its place is the problem of defending a particular pattern of adjustments for estimated risk (under this interpretation, the net-revenue-contributions approach could be criticized for assuming the same degree of risk in each period, without defending this assumption).

The usual suggestion for choice of a particular pattern of certainty equivalents is to employ management's estimates of the $R_j(t)$, as determined indirectly. Suppose that, for Year t, asset j's net-revenue contributions are estimated as $Y_j(t)$. Management might then be asked to reveal its utility preference as to risk by specifying the amount of a guaranteed *certain* cash receipt in Year t that would suffice to make it indifferent whether it received the guaranteed receipt or took its chances with asset j in that year. Call this guaranteed cash receipt $G_j(t)$. Then the certainty equivalent coefficient $R_j(t) = G_j(t)/Y_j(t)$. This changes the net-revenue contributions relationship to:

$$K_j = \sum_{t=1}^{N} \frac{[G_j(t)/Y_j(t)] \cdot Y_j(t)}{(1 + i)^t} = \sum_{t=1}^{N} \frac{G_j(t)}{(1 + i)^t}$$

---

[18] The following discussion is based in part on James C. Van Horne, *Financial Management and Policy* (Englewood Cliffs, New Jersey: Prentice-Hall, Inc., 1968), pp. 66–69; see also Andrew D. Bailey, Jr., and Jack Gray, "A Study of the Importance of the Planning Horizon on Reports Utilizing Discounted Future Cash Flows," *Journal of Accounting Research*, VI (Spring, 1968), 101–102.

Two questions would have to be answered, though, before this approach could be considered to be theoretically justified.

1. How can the use of *management's* utility preferences as to risk be defended? (The utility preferences of the *external* reader would seem more appropriate—but of course these would vary from reader to reader, leading to the same ambiguity as before.) If we do look to management's utility preferences, haven't we merely pushed the problem back one further step, without really solving it? How significantly does such an appeal differ from systematizing the accountant's present approach, which is to ask management what its *depreciation pattern* preferences are?[19]

2. As outlined above, the certainty equivalent approach involves an implicit assumption that the $R_j(t)$ should be calculated as independent magnitudes for each year. But actually, of course, the $R_j(t)$ interact. We have seen why there are an unlimited number of possible patterns of $r_j(t)$. For parallel reasons, there are an unlimited number of possible patterns of $R_j(t)$. This is easy to verify as soon as we recognize that there are an unlimited number of patterns of guaranteed cash receipts that would make management indifferent as to whether it received guaranteed cash or took its chances with the investment in asset *j as a whole*. Therefore, in this sense too, the certainty equivalents approach just pushes the problem back an extra step, without solving it.

Appendix B

Ambiguities in the Amortization of Bond Discount

It was suggested earlier that incidental investments in securities might escape the kinds of problems that have been discussed since Chapter Two. But this will not necessarily be true. For example, there is no method of recording interest revenue on investments in long-term debt, or interest expense on long-term debt obligations, that is theoretically justified *a priori*. Since the two problems are symmetrical, this will be illustrated as a problem in the amortization of discount on bonds payable.

For simplicity, suppose that a company issues a single 6 percent, 5-year bond with interest payable annually. The bond is sold for $979.22, to yield $6\frac{1}{2}$ percent annual interest. Over the bond's life there will be five interest payments of $60.00 each, for a total of $300.00. In addition, the company must pay $20.78 more at maturity than it received upon issue, raising the total interest expense over the bond's 5-year life to $320.78. Present accounting rules allow this $320.78 to be allocated to the five different years in either of two ways.

1. The company may employ a straight-line allocation, of $320.78/5 = \$64.156$ per year. This straight-line allocation is reflected in Table 5-5.

2. The company may employ a "compound interest" calculus that offers a constant $6\frac{1}{2}$ percent-per-year return on the bondholder's investment, as it gradually rises from $979.22 to the maturity value of $1,000.00. The details of this method, which is reflected in Table 5-6, may be found in various accounting texts.

---

[19] Another way to phrase the same question is to ask how significantly does this approach differ from the probabilistic version of the discounted-contributions approach developed in Allan R. Drebin, "Accounting for Proprietary Research," *Accounting Review*, XLI (July, 1966), 413–25?

TABLE 5-5

STRAIGHT-LINE AMORTIZATION OF BOND DISCOUNT

Year	Cash Payment	Amortization of Discount	Interest Expense for Year	Investment (Beginning-of-Year Book Value)	Current Year Rate of Return
1........	$60.000	$4.156	$ 64.156	$979.220	6.55%
2........	60.000	4.156	64.156	983.376	6.52%
3........	60.000	4.156	64.156	987.532	6.50%
4........	60.000	4.156	64.156	991.688	6.47%
5........	60.000	4.156	64.156	995.844	6.44%
			$320.780		

TABLE 5-6

COMPOUND-INTEREST AMORTIZATION OF BOND DISCOUNT

Year	Cash Payment	Amortization of Discount	Interest Expense for Year	Investment (Beginning-of-Year Book Value)	Current Year Rate of Return
1........	$60.000	$3.649	$ 63.649	$979.220	6.50%
2........	60.000	3.886	63.886	982.869	6.50%
3........	60.000	4.139	64.139	986.755	6.50%
4........	60.000	4.408	64.408	990.894	6.50%
5........	60.000	4.695	64.695	995.302	6.50%
			$320.777		

A number of authors have argued that, from a theoretical standpoint, the second of these allocation methods is preferable to the first because it gives a constant current-year rate of return on the bondholder's investment. But the arguments since Chapter One imply that *a priori* there is no more reason to favor equal annual return on investment here than with depreciable assets. The $6\frac{1}{2}$ percent *average* rate of return over the entire 5-year bond contract is compatible with any number of current-year rate of return patterns. For example, it is compatible with the decelerated recognition of interest expense reflected in Table 5-7. This particular pattern involves reverse sum-of-the-years'-digits amortization of the bond discount.

TABLE 5-7

DECELERATED AMORTIZATION OF BOND DISCOUNT

Year	Cash Payment	Amortization of Discount	Interest Expense for Year	Investment (Beginning-of-Year Book Value)	Current Year Rate of Return
1....	$60.000	$1.385	$ 61.385	$979.220	6.27%
2....	60.000	2.771	62.771	980.605	6.40%
3....	60.000	4.156	64.156	983.376	6.52%
4....	60.000	5.541	65.541	987.532	6.64%
5....	60.000	6.927	66.927	993.073	6.74%
			$320.780		

These comments are *not* offered to urge decelerated amortization of bond discount[20] (though it gives a pattern of annual interest rates that corresponds well with the general tendency of interest rates *ceteris paribus* to be higher on long-lived contracts than on short-lived contracts). Instead, the point is merely that there seems no way conclusively to defend *any* pattern chosen against all alternatives. Therefore any pattern will be arbitrary.

The argument is easily extended to premiums, and to *investments* in debt.

---

[20] But compare Ralph W. Snyder, "Approximate Amortization of Bond Premiums by 'Payments Outstanding' (or 'Sum of Digits') Method," *Accounting Review*, XXXIV (April, 1959), 182–94.

CHAPTER SIX

Some Possible Responses to the Problem

CHAPTER Five concluded that no solution to financial accounting's allocation problem exists within present allocation theory and conventional allocation rules. Since this problem is quite pervasive, there is no theoretically justified way to support most of the figures now appearing on financial statements. But there still remains a question of what to do *about* this problem, of how best to respond to it. An obvious partial answer is for theorists to direct research towards improving allocation theory. Certain earlier observations could be rephrased by saying that one reason accounting allocations are arbitrary is that theorists have made little serious effort to adapt allocation theory to the level of disaggregation required in conventional accounting. Once this effort is made, some better method of allocation may be developed, perhaps one that can cope with the interactions with which the financial accountant is faced. The discussions in Chapters One and Five have suggested other areas for research, too: can agreement be reached on the proper nature and priority of accounting goals? Can a theory of appropriate behavior under ignorance be developed? or a theory of choice among arbitrary alternatives?

But such research will take time—especially in view of the empirical difficulties mentioned at the end of the last chapter. What is to be done meanwhile? There seem to be two main choices.

1. Accountants may wish to remain within the present framework of conventional rules. In that case, they should explicitly recognize that their allocations are generally arbitrary, and respond in appropriate ways to that awareness. It will be suggested that an appropriate response here involves more uniformity in financial statements than is presently demanded. It also, of course, requires greater tolerance of arbitrariness than may be possessed by the public.

2. Accountants may wish to adopt one of the *un*conventional approaches to reporting economic activity that presently are being proposed by theorists.[1] Most of the unconventional approaches either fall into the same allocation problems as do the conventional ones, or lead to severe difficulties of their own. But the current-price valuation approaches recommended by Chambers and Sterling *can* be employed in a way that escapes the allocation problem. The resulting approach has other serious drawbacks, but nevertheless looks promising. Another way to escape the allocation problem would be to stop trying to measure income, and to prepare funds statements instead; this approach also seems promising. Finally, one might appeal to the beliefs of laymen, but, as will be demonstrated, this approach leads to results that seem to be unsatisfactory.

What should be emphasized here is that the essential thing for accountants to recognize is that if the arguments made in the previous chapters are correct, *some* kind

---

[1] The reader should not be misled by most of five chapters being devoted to conventional accounting approaches, while only part of one chapter is given up to unconventional approaches. No slighting of the unconventional approaches is either intended or involved. (In fact, my interest in the general problem of allocation stems in part from my having been converted in gradual succession to most of the unconventional methods discussed; far from being indifferent to them, I have the intense feelings of a former believer.) The only reason that the discussion of unconventional approaches is brief is that we now have the tools to discuss them efficiently.

of response is required (and that if these arguments are *not* correct, then they should be explicitly refuted).

I. The General Problem of Income Determination

By now it should be evident to the reader that the choice of an appropriate response to the allocation problem is just one aspect of the more general problem of what approach to income determination should be taken in financial accounting.[2] Much of financial accounting theory in the last 75 or so years is essentially a prolonged effort to give operational content to economists' theoretical notions of income. Without tracing the historical development of this effort, we can identify two main approaches (with numerous sub-approaches) that theorists have used.[3]

Appraisal approaches[4]

One school of theorists follows an appraisal approach to income determination. The entity's assets and liabilities are valued at the end of the year. The totals are compared with totals calculated in a similar manner at the beginning of the year. Net income for the year is the difference between these two sets of magnitudes. Letting Y represent income, A represent assets, L liabilities, and subscripts refer to successive points in time, we have the following familiar equation:

$$Y_{(0,1)} = (A_1 - L_1) - (A_0 - L_0).$$

Different accounting theorists have suggested several different kinds of appraisal approaches.

1. One approach entered accounting theory from the writings of Irving Fisher and his disciples; more recently it has been reflected in the writings of such authors as Alexander, Moonitz, Storey, and Zeff.[5] These authors recommend various forms of

---

[2] As Sprouse correctly observed, an earlier work of mine on revenues left the whole income determination question up in the air. See Robert T. Sprouse, review, *Accounting Review*, XLII (July, 1967), 631–32. This omission was deliberate: as this chapter demonstrates, a discussion confined to revenues avoids many of the problems that a discussion of income must consider (and traditionally accountants *do* discuss the two problems separately). But ultimately of course the income problem must also be faced; that is what this study attempts to do.

In turn, this study avoids discussion of the implications that its conclusions have for allocations in cost accounting, for transfer pricing, for cost justification (and other problems stemming from governmental regulation of industry), for taxation, for goodwill and the business combinations controversy, and generally for any other situations in which the accountant or the regulatory authority wishes to assign portions of an acquisition price to different assets, time periods, or activities. It is likely that many of the main practical applications of this study lie in these directions. But one thing at a time must suffice.

[3] There is a good discussion of these approaches, particularly of what I call the "appraisal" approaches in Robert R. Sterling, "The Theory of the Measurement of the Income of Trading Enterprises" (unpublished doctoral dissertation, University of Florida, 1965 [forthcoming from the University Press of Kansas]) Chapters I, VIII, IX; for a discussion that employs a different scheme of organization from the one used here, see Eldon S. Hendriksen, *Accounting Theory* (Homewood, Illinois: Richard D. Irwin, Inc., 1965), Chapters 5 and 6. Hendriksen distinguishes between "capital maintenance concepts" of income, which require valuation, and a "transactions approach," which requires matching—this is particularly clearly expressed on p. 192. This distinction dovetails with the ones employed in what follows.

[4] For simplicity, the rest of this chapter will assume annual financial statements, that there are no additions or withdrawals of capital by the owners of the enterprise, and that there are no non-operating gains or losses. Finally, cases in which revenues result from discharge of liabilities will be disregarded. This is merely to speed the discussion along; the reader should satisfy himself that these simplifications do not affect the conclusions reached.

[5] See Sidney S. Alexander, "Income Measurement in a Dynamic Economy," revised by David Solomons, in W. T. Baxter and Sidney Davidson, editors, *Studies in Accounting Theory* (Homewood, Illinois: Richard D.

discounted-contributions valuation—of appraisal in terms of the discounted present values of the firm's estimated future net-revenue contributions (or cash flows). This approach will be discussed in section II of this chapter.

2. Another approach, reflected in the reports of various committees of the American Accounting Association and in the writings of Chambers and Sterling,[6] recommends that these appraisals be made in terms of one or another of the various kinds of current-price valuation approaches. These approaches are also discussed in section II of this chapter.

Matching approaches

The other main approach to income determination is the one traditionally followed in accounting practice—the matching approach.[7] A magnitude called "total revenues" is calculated. This magnitude reflects the total cash and claims to receive cash that have been obtained from customers during the year (as a result of the firm's supplying services or products). From total revenues are subtracted various expense magnitudes representing either:

1. The costs of assets given up or liabilities incurred to supply these services or products (for example, salaries expense); or

2. An allocation of costs, where the total cost is deemed to benefit the activities of more than one year (for example, depreciation expense). The details of this are described in Chapter One; as we have seen, *both* kinds of expenses involve allocations of nonmonetary economic goods, though in the first case the allocation is to the economic activity of a single year. Letting Y represent income again, R total revenues, and E total expenses, and subscripts refer again to successive points in time, we have the familiar alternative equation:

$$Y_{(0,1)} = R_{(0,1)} - E_{(0,1)}$$

These matching approaches will be discussed in section III of this chapter.

Finally, there is a good deal of promising research being done in measurement science, communication theory, and the behavioral sciences[8]—research that may

---

Irwin, Inc., 1962), pp. 126–200; Maurice Moonitz and Louis H. Jordan, *Accounting, An Analysis of its Problems*, Revised Edition (New York: Holt, Rinehart and Winston, Inc., 1963), Vol. I, Chapter 5; Reed K. Storey "Cash Movements and Periodic Income Determination," *Accounting Review*, XXXV (July, 1960), 449–54; and Stephen A. Zeff, "Replacement Cost: Member of the Family, Welcome Guest, or Intruder?" *Accounting Review*, XXXVII (October, 1962), 611–25.

[6] "Accounting for Land, Buildings, and Equipment," *Accounting Review*, XXXIX (July, 1964), 693–99; "A Discussion of Various Approaches to Inventory Measurement," *Accounting Review*, XXXIX (July, 1964), 700–14; "The Realization Concept," *Accounting Review*, XL (April, 1965), 312–22; "The Matching Concept," *Accounting Review*, XL (April, 1965), 368–72; Raymond J. Chambers, *Accounting, Evaluation and Economic Behavior* (Englewood Cliffs, New Jersey: Prentice-Hall, Inc., 1966); and Sterling (1965).

[7] Actually, as Chapter One indicates, both an "attaching" and a "matching" process are involved here, since the costs of many goods are allocated to the costs of one or more *other* goods before any matching with revenue is done.

[8] Here are some recent examples from the literature. The following is not intended as a complete bibliography, and some works overlap categories—Chambers (1966) is a good example of such overlap.

Measurement Science. See Carl Thomas Devine, *Essays in Accounting Theory* (privately printed, 1962); Harold Bierman, Jr., "Measurement and Accounting," *Accounting Review*, XXXVIII (July, 1963), 501–507; Richard Mattessich, *Accounting and Analytical Methods* (Homewood, Illinois: Richard D. Irwin, Inc., 1964); R. J. Chambers, "Measurement and Objectivity in Accounting," *Accounting Review*, XXXIX (April, 1964), 264–74; Ronald S. Lim, "The Mathematical Propriety of Accounting Measurements and Calculations," *Accounting Review*, XLI (October, 1966), 642–51; Yuji Ijiri and Robert K. Jaedicke, "Reliability and Objectivity of Accounting Measurements," *Accounting Review*, XLI (July, 1966), 474–83; Yuji Ijiri, *The Foundations of*

eventually lead to additional approaches to income measurement. But none of these research efforts have yet reached the point where they can be regarded as responses to the accountant's allocation problem, and they will not be discussed in what follows.

II. Unconventional Approaches to Income Measurement

Compressed reports[9]

One way to avoid the allocation problem within years was mentioned earlier. If one combines reported data enough, a point eventually will be reached at which the aggregated revenue function contains no within-year input interactions. If we assume that the investor should be concerned to estimate an over-all *average* rate of return on the firm's invested capital, then the problem of defending a particular pattern of within-year implicit rates also is avoided.

It could be argued that financial accounting needs a method which permits the best prediction in an acceptable investors' model. If the long-run internal rate of return is a good predictor, perhaps financial statements should be prepared in such a way that they report a constant rate of return over time (except as changes exterior to the firm alter expectations).[10] Compressed financial statements would be consistent with this and, at some level of aggregation, it might be possible to justify any related allocations. (An important practical question, outside the concern of this study, is whether the necessary estimates could be made reliably enough for such compressed statements to be worth preparation. Could probabilistic estimates be made, so as to generate ranges instead of the usual point estimates? If the investor should be interested in estimating an average rate of return, should he not be equally interested in

---

Accounting Measurement (Englewood Cliffs, New Jersey: Prentice-Hall, Inc., 1967); Daniel L. McDonald, "Feasibility Criteria for Accounting Measures," *Accounting Review*, XLII (October, 1967), 662–79, and "A Test Application of the Feasibility of Market Based Measures in Accounting," *Journal of Accounting Research*, VI (Spring, 1968), 38–49.

Communication Theory. See Norton M. Bedford and Vahe Baladouni, "A Communication Theory Approach to Accountancy," *Accounting Review*, XXXVII (October, 1962), 650–59; and David H. Li, "The Semantic Aspect of Communication Theory and Accountancy," *Journal of Accounting Research*, I (Spring, 1963), 102–107.

Behavioral Science. See Edwin H. Caplan, "Behavioral Assumptions of Management Accounting," *Accounting Review*, XLI (July, 1966), 496–509; Reginald S. Gynther, "Accounting Concepts and Behavioral Hypotheses," *Accounting Review*, XLII (April, 1967), 274–90; Jacob G. Birnberg and Raghu Nath, "Implications of Behavioral Science for Managerial Accounting," *Accounting Review*, XLII (July, 1967), 468–79; and Edwin H. Caplan, "Behavioral Assumptions of Management Accounting—Report of a Field Study," *Accounting Review*, XLIII (April, 1968), pp. 342–62.

General. See Myron J. Gordon, "Postulates, Principles and Research in Accounting," *Accounting Review*, XXXIX (April, 1964), 251–63; Myron J. Gordon, Bertrand N. Horwitz, and Philip T. Meyers, "Accounting Measurements and Normal Growth of the Firm," in Robert K. Jaedicke, Yuji Ijiri, and Oswald Nielsen, editors, *Research in Accounting Measurement* (Evanston, Illinois: American Accounting Association, 1966), 221–31; and Michael Schiff, "Accounting Tactics and the Theory of the Firm," *Journal of Accounting Research*, IV (Spring, 1966), 62–67.

[9] For background to this subsection, see Carl Thomas Devine, "The Unit Problem," in Devine (1962), pp. 201–16.

[10] Actually, there are two possibilities here.

a) It may be that the long-run rate of return is a good predictor. If so, financial statements should be prepared in such a way that this average rate is discernable.

b) However, it may be that investors should be following a kind of Bayesian approach, constantly tracking the moving target of the firm's long-run *future* average rate of return (this is the interpretation that I personally prefer).

The degree of smoothing done will differ under these two goals. Under the second, the reader needs data about fluctuations in the rate in order to make successive adjustments toward approximating the long-run rate.

the extent to which his estimates might err?) Unfortunately, this approach does not look very promising.

1. While it avoids defense of a particular pattern of within-year implicit rates of return, it seems subject to the various other problems of allocations *among* years that were discussed in Chapter Five.

2. As has been argued before, drastic compression would be necessary before the revenue function no longer incorporated within-year interaction effects. It is hard to see how such compression could stop short of having almost all unexpired nonmonetary economic goods reflected in a single figure on the balance sheet, and almost all expirations of such goods reflected in a single expense figure on the income statement. Devine's comments seem very appropriate here:

A second glance is likely to reduce optimism over the expected benefits of an overall enterprise approach. What are the rules for anticipating, estimating and especially measuring future favorable and unfavorable events? It might be possible to make such estimates without regard to the existing pile of *individual* resources and the necessity for replenishing and perhaps expanding the pile, but clearly estimates must be tied to manageable factors that seem to have relevance to the future stream of events. Overall estimates of this sort may be prepared for relatively uncomplicated activities, but most businessmen probably feel a need to examine the individual agents that contribute to the future events in some way that appeals to their intuitive feeling for cause and effect and for responsibility. Thus some attention to the individual agents contributing to the stream of favorable circumstances seems to be indicated. Certainly estimates of future expenditures for an entire enterprise must be related somehow to the services needed to preserve the revenue stream and the services required may conveniently be related to particular sources—assets and potentials for specific kinds of service. In other words our present estimating techniques usually proceed *from* specific services needed *to* expenditures required rather than directly to expenditures back to individual services necessary to support the income stream.[11]

What Devine says here of the businessman applies with equal force to *any* reader using financial statements for prediction.

There is one other way in which compression might be accomplished—one that partly avoids the previous difficulties. One might abandon annual reports for a kind of venture accounting, wherein reports would be prepared irregularly upon completion of major company projects.[12] Allocations would thereby be avoided if:

1. There were no continuing projects of indefinite length;

2. Costs common to two or more projects were negligible, and ventures did not interact.

Unfortunately, neither of these conditions is common. Nor is it likely that investors would be any more content with irregular reports than they would be with drastically compressed reports.

Discounted-contributions valuation

It should be obvious from the description of the approach (in Chapter Two), that discounted-contributions valuation suffers from exactly the same difficulties as does the net-revenue-contributions approach. Moreover, an additional ambiguity appears,

---

[11] Devine (1962), pp. 202–203.

[12] While it is not what Coughlan himself ends up recommending, this idea seems implicit in John Coughlan, "Industrial Accounting," *Accounting Review*, XXXIV (July, 1959), 415–28.

one discussed by Wright: four different approaches to calculating depreciation became possible, each of which can result in a different depreciation pattern.[13]

Despite the contrary belief of many accountants and economists, the discounted-contributions approach will be arbitrary unless the entity's revenue function does not incorporate interactions. But this will almost never be true, except possibly under the kind of drastic compression discussed in the previous subsection. Couple this with the widely admitted difficulty, uncertainty, and unreliability of the estimates required by this method, and one may conclude that, at present, discounted-contributions valuation just is not a promising approach to income determination, whatever may be its uses in capital budgeting and other decision making situations.[14]

Current-price approaches

From the standpoint of this study, the key question with the various current-price approaches is whether or not they avoid the necessity of making allocations. Hendriksen lists the following as part of his general discussion of asset valuation (what follows is a paraphrase).[15]

Input-value approaches (entry prices):

1. *Current input prices:* The costs, in today's prices, of acquiring the good in its present condition—or of acquiring an equivalent good embodying the same remaining services.
2. *Discounted future prices:* much the same as the current-input-prices approach except that the prices employed are estimates of what the remaining services

---

[13] See F. K. Wright, "Depreciation Theory and the Cost of Funds," *Accounting Review*, XXXVIII (January, 1963), 87–90. Wright uses the opportunity cost of funds as his rate of discount—as the rate of interest that should be earned on the investment in the depreciable asset. His "net contribution to period earnings" is what I have called the asset's net-revenue contributions, less the interest on the investment for the period. His "net period return" is the net contribution to period earnings, less depreciation (the net period return is zero when the discount rate equals the implicit interest rate, as it does under the net-revenue-contributions approach). Wright points out that two criteria must be chosen:
1. Should depreciation for the period be proportional to the net contribution to period earnings, or should the net period return be proportional to the investment in the asset?
2. Should the interest charged against the period be proportional to the depreciation charge for the period, or to the investment in the asset?
There are four possible combined decisions, each of which can result in a different depreciation pattern. And once again there seems no way conclusively to defend any one criterion against its alternative.
There is a related problem of allocation of purchaser's surplus which the use of the implicit rate avoids. One can argue from this point of view that use of the implicit rate (or, equivalently, use of the net-revenue-contributions approach) is an allocation decision itself—the effect of which is to allocate the purchaser's surplus in one of the infinite number of possible ways in which it might be allocated; compare Gabriel A. D. Preinreich, "Annual Survey of Economic Theory: The Theory of Depreciation," *Econometrica*, VI (July, 1938), 236–39.

[14] These comments also pertain to the limiting case of discounted-contributions valuation at a zero rate of discount—an approach employed in an initial stage of the argument used in Coughlan (1959) (see p. 417). For additional objections to discounted-contributions valuation, and the whole related concept of "economic income," see Keith Shwayder, "A Critique of Economic Income as an Accounting Concept," *Abacus*, III (August, 1967), 23–35.

[15] Hendriksen (1965), pp. 218–20. Hendriksen also discusses discounted-contributions valuation and conventional approaches in this part of his book. His analysis is made in terms of valuation and directed toward the balance sheet. But because of the close relationship between the balance sheet and the income statement, in effect his analysis is also a thorough discussion of the possible ways of writing off nonmonetary goods. Hendriksen also discusses valuation in terms of *un*discounted future net cash receipts (with inventories, this will be the net-realizable-values approach, for reasons that Hendriksen gives on pp. 249–51). As our previous discussion indicated, though, this latter approach leads to the same difficulties as the former.
For related discussions, see Hendriksen (1965), pp. 184–87, 203–204, 206–207, 248–56, 261–62.

of the asset will cost at the time they will be utilized (rather than their present cost), as discounted at some appropriate rate of return.

Output-value approaches (exit prices):

    3. *Current output values:* valuation in terms of the selling price of the good in the market in which the entity normally sells its product or service. This method is primarily intended as an inventory-valuation approach. (The outputs of depreciable assets extend over a number of years. So, for depreciable assets the current-output-values approach becomes a variant of either discounted-contributions valuation or the net-revenue-contributions approach, and accordingly suffers from the same allocation difficulties as conventional methods.)

    4. *Liquidation values:* similar to the current-output-values approach, except that the market considered is not the one in which the firm normally sells. Instead, the values are obtained from prices for second-hand goods (where such prices are available) and from estimates of prices that would be obtained in liquidation.

This is a valuable checklist. But for purposes of this study a different classification scheme is needed. The important thing to recognize is that few of the unconventional approaches mentioned above involve any allocation method that has not already been discussed in this study, though *what is allocated* differs. For example, most current-input-price methods substitute some other amount for the historical acquisition prices employed in conventional accounting. But this new magnitude is allocated according to the same methods that conventional accounting uses for *its* magnitudes.

Suppose that it is decided to report a partly depreciated machine at its replacement cost. There are several ways to do this. One of these involves determining the current price, new, of a similar machine, then adjusting that price for depreciation to date on the actual machine; another way is to adjust the machine's depreciated historical acquisition price by a price index calculated for machines of its type. *Obviously, such approaches to replacement cost valuation involve exactly the same allocation problems as does conventional accounting.* So does the approach that involves estimating the remaining services in the old machine, then determining the price of a used (or new) machine embodying the same services.

Similarly, if one is obtaining a replacement (entry) cost figure for a building, one does not intend to report a figure for a *new* building offering the same services as the present building offered when it was new. Instead, one intends to report a figure adjusted to reflect the present building's *remaining* services. But to do this one must determine a general depreciation pattern for the building, and this leads to exactly the same allocation problems as are experienced with conventional depreciation methods. Put this another way: the task of conventional depreciation is to find some pattern by which to allocate historical acquisition prices to different periods of time. Here, the current-cost valuation approaches just substitute present or future market prices for historical costs. This substitution does not affect the basic allocation problem one way or another.[16] Here are some more examples of unconventional approaches that lead to exactly the same allocation difficulties as conventional approaches:

---

[16] In addition, of course, the *discounted-future prices* approach suffers from any ambiguities associated with rates of return and with discounting.

Where there is no established market for assets of like kind and condition, current cost may be estimated by reference to the purchase price of assets which provide equivalent service capacity.[17]

In many cases the current cost of raw materials and labor should be determinable with tolerable precision by employing current wage rates and material costs multiplied by the actual (or standard) quantity of labor or material related to the partially or fully completed product. In the case of indirect manufacturing costs, adjustment of historical cost to current cost by the use of index numbers which give effect to changes in the price level of indirect cost factors may be the best available procedure.[18]

While the current value of the services of an asset are measured best by the current cost of equivalent services, such costs are usually not available or they are irrelevant because the acquisition of such services in small chunks is not the most efficient way of obtaining them. The best alternative is to obtain the current replacement cost of the asset and allocate a portion of this to the current period's operations. The current replacement cost less accumulated depreciation to date also provides a balance sheet estimate of the current value of the unused services to be provided by the asset.[19]

In some cases such allocation difficulties can be escaped—a current exit or entry price can be determined *without making any allocations*. This is particularly true of inventories. But it is also true of the kinds of land and depreciable assets for which there is an active second-hand market.[20] For example, if one owns a 1967 Detroit car showing no obvious defects, the price that it would command can be determined fairly accurately without one's having to make depreciation calculations. In effect the *market* makes the necessary allocations.[21]

But escaping allocation difficulties in this way does not merely require that there be an active second-hand market. It also requires that there be some way of determining that the asset owned is substantially identical with some other asset traded in the second-hand market, without any allocation being performed to determine this. Such equation of assets without allocation *is* possible for some kinds of assets; besides automobiles and inventories, sometimes it can be determined, say, that two buildings are similar with respect to size, materials, location, state of repair, and so forth—in which case the market price of one may be used as a basis for estimating a current price for the other. Call this process of equation-of-two-assets-without-allocation *direct equation*.

Unfortunately, there are a number of durables (specialized durables or durables

---

[17] AAA (Land), p. 695; see also the discussion of depreciation on pp. 695–97.

[18] AAA (Inventory), p. 710, quoted approvingly in AAA (Realization), p. 321.

[19] Hendriksen (1965), pp. 292–93. See the discussion on pp. 292–96, generally.

[20] See AAA (Land), p. 695.

[21] The question might be raised whether this appeal to the market doesn't merely push the problem back another stage: why is it theoretically justifiable for the *market* to make the allocations? Yet here is a case where presumably both laymen and economists would agree that market prices are appropriate. As we saw in Chapter One, whatever the purpose of accounting should be, it includes reporting on economic activity—activity of the kind that takes place in markets. An ultimate appeal to market valuation is consistent with this purpose.

Contrast the following suggestion, which does *not* seem pertinent. One might value a machine for which there was no active second-hand market by searching for some second-hand asset such that management would be indifferent between possessing that second-hand asset and the one now owned. The magnitude associated with the asset now owned would then be set equal to the current price of the second-hand asset.

This approach does simply push the problem back a stage—much as the certainty equivalents approach did in the appendix to Chapter Five. An appeal to *management's* valuations is not conclusive to either laymen or economists . . . and the problem becomes one of how to justify whatever allocations implicitly or explicitly undergird management's valuations.

lacking active second-hand markets) for which direct equation will be impossible. More generally (and what follows is the basic classification that has been sought in this subsection) some nonmonetary assets are subject to direct equation with other assets, but the valuation of other nonmonetary assets requires allocations. Similarly, some current-price methods aim at direct equation of nonmonetary assets; others do not. If a current-price method uses direct equation of nonmonetary assets it will thereby escape the allocation problems discussed in this study. If it does not, the current-price method will be subject to all the allocation difficulties of conventional accounting.[22]

Chambers' and Sterling's approaches

If my interpretations are correct, the "continuously contemporary accounting" proposed by Chambers and the current-price valuation measurements proposed by Sterling are attempts to ground financial statement magnitudes firmly in direct equation and unallocated current market prices.[23] Unfortunately, direct equation is impossible for many assets, including all those that Chambers calls "nonvendible durables."[24] Various ways of obtaining surrogate magnitudes in lieu of direct-equation market values might be suggested for such assets. But all of these ways involve allocations of the kinds we are trying to avoid. For instance, one might estimate the current market value of a used machine by determining the cost of equivalent service potential from a new machine, or by applying an index of new machine prices to the depreciated historical acquisition price of the old machine . . . or by following any of the other methods previously mentioned that employ allocations. But, as we have seen, all of these approaches lead to arbitrary results.

This point is stressed because Chambers avails himself of a number of such surrogates.[25] While one can sympathize with the reasons that he gives for doing so, his appeal to surrogates destroys a major virtue of his approach—that it escapes the allocation problem by not allocating.[26]

If we do not use surrogates, what then? The answer that would be the most consistent within Chamber's own system would be to report goods for which direct-equation market values are unobtainable at a zero magnitude. (Chambers seems to consider reporting nonvendible durables at small, non-zero values—net realizable values at a forced sale, for example—but this must involve direct equation, allocation, or both together.) However, employing zero magnitudes still involves allocation—in this

---

[22] The possibility of allocating the entire cost to the year of acquisition will be examined below.

[23] See Chambers (1966) and Sterling (1965). Chambers' book is, of course, the more familiar at present; Sterling's reaches similar conclusions by a different route. Since Sterling's book is presently both difficult to obtain and undergoing revision, the following remarks are confined to Chambers' work.

[24] Chambers (1966), p. 243. See also Robert T. Sprouse and Maurice Moonitz, *A Tentative Set of Broad Accounting Principles for Business Enterprises* (New York: American Institute of Certified Public Accountants, 1962), p. 33.

[25] For example, see Chambers (1966), pp. 242–51; R. J. Chambers, "Measurement in Accounting", *Journal of Accounting Research*, III (Spring, 1965), p. 57; and R. J. Chambers, *Towards a General Theory of Accounting* (Adelaide, Australia: The University of Adelaide, 1961), pp. 28–29, 37–38.

[26] There is an excellent discussion of Chambers' efforts to employ surrogates in F. K. Wright, "Capacity for Adaptation and the Asset Measurement Problem," *Abacus*, III (August, 1967), 74–79. Iselin charges that this use of surrogates is inconsistent, and that under Chambers' system net realizable values should be used in measuring all assets—see Errol R. Iselin, "Chambers on Accounting Theory," *Accounting Review*, XLIII (April, 1968), 233; see also Chambers' reply: R. J. Chambers, "Measures and Values," *Accounting Review*, XLIII (April, 1968), 247. But it is even more important that only by consistent use of direct-equation market values does Chambers' system avoid the allocation problem. His use of surrogates is unfortunate chiefly because it discards a major advantage of his system.

case allocation of the entire acquisition price to the activities of the year of purchase. Chambers tries to justify this as a correct reflection of the decrease in decision-making flexibility resulting from buying the asset. For example:

> A firm which makes outlays on specialized, nonvendible goods forecloses the opportunity of adapting itself by resale of those goods . . . There seem, therefore, to be grounds for assigning no current cash equivalent to them.[27]

Another possible response is the one considered in the next section: the problem of the proper treatment of goods for which direct-equation market values are unobtainable arises because the accountant is trying to measure *income*. The measuring of *funds flows* does not encounter this particular problem: acquisition of the related goods unambiguously involves current expenditures of known amounts of funds. This, as we shall see, suggests the possibility of abandoning the income-measurement effort.

Chambers might well argue that his surrogate magnitudes, whatever their deficiencies, were preferable to historical costs. But unless one or the other approach *must* be used, this is not an argument for the use of surrogates, but only for *not* using historical costs. We might use neither. Arguments of the form "this method is preferable to that method" are irrelevant to a critique that questions whether *any* method need be employed.

Other difficulties with Chambers' approach

In the rest of this discussion I will consider Chambers' approach in its "pure" form, without surrogates—for it is in this form that it offers a way to avoid the allocation problem. Goods for which direct-equation market values are available will be reported at these values; other goods will be reported at zero. Even so, there still will be a number of difficulties associated with Chambers' approach.

1. *Level of aggregation of market values.* It is not immediately obvious at what level of aggregation these market values should be calculated. Using the second-hand market for equipment as an example, the possibilities range along a continuum from valuing each good individually to determining a single market value for the firm as a "going concern."[28]

This problem has been pointed out by Larson and Schattke.[29] The total of the amounts that purchasers will pay for assets individually does not necessarily equal the amount that these goods would command if sold as a group or as parts of a going concern. And on first impression this observation seems to lead to the same kinds of problems of joint determination that have troubled us all along. To use Larson and Schattke's own example, imagine two assets whose market values if sold individually are $10 and $15. If these assets

> . . . were combined and placed on the market as one package, the realizable price of the

---

[27] Chambers (1966), p. 243; the observation is also based on personal conversations with Chambers in February, 1967.

[28] This last possibility has become increasingly plausible in recent years as more and more large companies have engaged in conglomerate diversification. It may well be that stockholders of all but the very largest companies should be trying to estimate what their company might bring if sold as a going concern.

[29] Kermit Larson and R. W. Schattke, "Current Cash Equivalent, Additivity, and Financial Action," *Accounting Review*, XLI (October, 1966), 634–41; Kermit D. Larson, "Descriptive Validity of Accounting Calculations," *Accounting Review*, XLII (July, 1967), 480–88.

combination may be more or less than $25. Furthermore, it would be largely a matter of coincidence if the realizable price of the combination were $25.[30]

The effect of this objection is that the notion of the current market price of the good becomes ambiguous for the same reason that the notion of a good's net-revenue contributions is ambiguous: assets interact. (Moreover, it could be urged that in particular the valuation of a firm in terms of what its goods would command individually has exactly the defects of allocation by the marginal contribution made by the last unit.)

Chambers' reply to this[31] can be summarized as follows. First, were the price of the combination *less* than $25, they would be sold individually; any combined price that is less than the totals at some lower level of aggregation is simply irrelevant. More generally, amounts reported for assets should reflect rational management behavior under present conditions. Management should know approximately the level of aggregation at which goods could most profitably be sold. For some goods this would involve sale in isolation; for others it would involve sale in combination. The market values associated with goods should be whichever market values are consistent with such rational calculations. This approach is permissible because financial statements report somewhat aggregated figures anyway.

Chambers himself is not entirely consistent with this reply. In the article cited he speaks of choosing market values on at least two other bases. One might simply choose those that are the most likely to be encountered. Or one might argue that the market values that would be realized if assets were sold individually are as appropriate as any others (an argument which is at best what I have called a partial defense).[32] In his book he seems in places to envision conventional cost accounting allocations entering the market value calculations for inventories (unless their total is higher than the net realizable value).[33] None of this will be satisfactory. But if Chambers restricts himself to the position summarized above and his approach is used in its "pure" form, he may possibly escape both the allocation problem *and* these ambiguities of aggregation.

However, we have seen before that an appeal to management's opinions is not usually a way to obtain theoretical justification for magnitudes reported on financial statements. To put this point in terms that are consistent with Chambers' own arguments, the reported magnitudes will depend in part upon management's expectations of which marketing strategy will maximize proceeds. Chambers makes a point of rejecting valuation in terms of estimated future cash flows or estimated future market values, on the grounds that accounting should be a measurement system, and estimates just aren't measurements. But are magnitudes that depend on market-strategy estimates measurements either?

The problem of the level of aggregation at which current prices should be calculated remains troublesome; though it seems likely that some solution to it will eventually be found.

2. *Exit versus entry prices.* There is a similar problem for which an eventual solu-

---

[30] Larson and Schattke (1966), p. 639.

[31] R. J. Chambers, "Continuously Contemporary Accounting—Additivity and Action," *Accounting Review*, XLII (October, 1967), 751–57.

[32] Chambers (1967), p. 754.

[33] Chambers (1966), p. 232.

tion also seems likely. Chambers appears willing to choose either exit or entry prices for his current-price valuations, depending upon which approach leads to fewer difficulties.[34] But (as anyone who has traded in a car knows) there can be a large spread between entry and exit prices for the same good. This spread reaches its maximum with durables, but it will be present with any good whose market is characterized by certain imperfections.[35] It will be necessary to develop some theoretically justified way of deciding whether exit or entry prices are to be used for goods where direct-equation market values can be calculated—otherwise there will be substantial ambiguity in Chambers' approach.

3. *Conflict with present practice.* Chambers' approach, in its "pure" form without surrogates, represents a radical departure from present accounting practice—so radical that many will feel that his approach *avoids* rather than solves the problem of determining income. For example, suppose that this year a company buys a new, highly specialized, plant at a cost several times its average net income for the past few years. Suppose also that there is no potential purchaser for the company as a whole. The second-hand (break-up) market value of such a plant is apt to be very low. If so, *ceteris paribus* any current-price valuation approach that avoided the allocation problem by determining an unallocated direct-equation market price from a second-hand market would report a large net loss for the year in which the plant was acquired. Perhaps a logical defense can be offered by doing this. Certainly a case can be made for reporting such second-hand market information to investors and to management. But the resulting income magnitude seems far removed from what laymen, most accountants, and most economists generally mean by income. As Hendriksen comments,

. . the net income would be similar to that which would be obtained if the firm were liquidated at the end of each period and then started over with the liquidation valuations for the next period.[36]

If much financial accounting has been an effort to give operational significance to economists' theoretical notions of income, and if *this* is the best that accountants presently can do, will not most readers conclude that the accountants' efforts have failed?[37] To be sure, the existence of a conflict tells us nothing about who is right. But merely being right is not enough; if Chambers *is* right, he must alter the basic ways in which most readers perceive the income problem. This, one gathers, he is endeavoring to do.

---

[34] For a clear-cut instance of this, see Chambers (1965), pp. 54–56.

[35] There is a good discussion of this problem in G. Edward Philips, "The Revolution in Accounting Theory," *Accounting Review*, XXXVIII (October, 1963), 707.

[36] Hendriksen (1965), p. 107.

[37] Speaking of the same problem of nonvendible durables under Chambers' system, Solomons comments:

"Such assets would generally be highly specific to a particular business but might, of course, be excellent investments nevertheless. Since these assets have no alternative use outside the business, holding them involves no opportunity cost, and in Chambers's view, recognition of their zero resale value must force the business to recognize a loss of residual equity as soon as such an asset has been bought. Yet clearly the asset would not have been bought if the business had thought of the purchase as involving a loss. The use of resale prices in this situation leads to what I can only regard as an absurdity and a flagrant failure to measure up to the criterion of correspondence with the economic events which are being recorded."

—David Solomons, review of Chambers (1966), *Abacus*, II (December, 1966), 208. One might add that this case of nonvendible durables is only an extreme instance of something that would be relatively common under Chambers' system. See also Wright (1967).

4. *Problems of interaction.* Finally, it seems inane to try to determine market values for certain major kinds of nonmonetary assets. As an extreme example, of what possible significance to any management or investor decision is the market value of the land underneath, say, a major plant complex of an automobile company? Not only would the company have to relocate the plant in order to sell the land, but if it *did* move elsewhere and sell the land, the very decision to relocate would completely disrupt local land values! Chambers (and Sterling) both argue quite effectively that traditional accounting rules for reporting nonmonetary assets generate figures that have little decision significance. But the same can be said of many current market values.

More generally, if goods are to be assigned current market values, these goods must be severable from the firm. But some goods interact so complexly with other inputs (and with the environment in which the firm operates) that the consequences of severing them from the firm cannot be specified. As with so many other matters discussed in this study, interactions defeat what one would like to accomplish.

The approach recommended by Chambers and Sterling looks promising. But at present all that it offers is promise. It cannot yet be regarded as a solution to the problems of allocation and income determination.

Other current-price approaches

Other current-price approaches developed to date offer less promise; a few should be mentioned, though. The accountant might estimate what it would have cost to have *rented* the services of the firm's nonmonetary assets for a year. This amount could be regarded as the depreciation charge for the year. Remaining service lives could be estimated and multiplied by either present or estimated future annual rental fees, and the results discounted to obtain figures for the balance sheet (a zero discount rate could be employed if use of a positive rate led to any serious problems). This avoids the allocation problem. But it does so by assuming away another kind of interaction, similar to that pointed out by Larson and Schattke: presumably the cost of the services to the company (as owner of the asset combination) should be less than the total costs of these services rented individually. The essence of ownership is that one is *not* renting—why make contrary-to-fact assumptions? Edwards and Bell make a similar suggestion:

If historic cost is to be allocated among the asset's services as time passes, it is necessary to know in advance the total stock of these services. Otherwise there can be no basis for apportionment. Current cost depreciation, on the other hand, requires in theory no such clairvoyance. We need only know the services used or foregone this period and the price this period of those services. A truly open-ended approach to the life of a fixed asset is therefore conceivable.[38]

If this implies determining the current *rental* price of these services, then the previous remarks apply. However, it might imply something else. The accountant could inquire into the prices that assets offering similar services were selling for, then divide this amount by their service lives to determine the cost of one year's service. But this, of course, leads to exactly the kinds of difficulties first discussed in Chapter Two—why an equal allocation to each year?

---

[38] Edgar O. Edwards and Philip W. Bell, *The Theory and Measurement of Business Income* (Berkeley: The University of California Press, 1961), p. 175.

Hybrid methods

Naturally, the conclusions reached regarding the foregoing methods pertain to any attempt to combine these methods—whether by treating one as a surrogate for another (as so often is done with current input prices and discounted-contributions valuation), or otherwise. One of the most interesting hybrid approaches has been suggested by F. K. Wright.[39] Wright argues that the value-in-use of an asset is measured by the least costly of the alternatives avoided by owning the asset. These alternatives may be divided into two groups:

1. *Utilities:* the cheapest alternative involving giving up the kind of services provided by the asset.

2. *Replacement costs:* the cheapest alternative involving acquiring these kinds of services in some other way. Under his "least costly alternative" approach, the value-in-use of an asset would be the lower of its utility or replacement cost.

Determination of the asset's replacement cost involves all the problems that plague the current-price valuation approaches. Determination of utilities, in Wright's sense, will be possible only so long as interaction effects are not present or can be ignored. But, of course, this is exactly what the arguments in Chapters Three through Five indicate will not usually be true.[40]

In summary, any current-price valuation approach will be a possible response to the allocation problem *if it avoids making allocations.* But most current-price approaches allocate (and those that do not have *other* problems with interactions).

III. Matching Approaches

It is entirely possible that under conventional matching approaches, much the same problems arise in allocating *revenues and gains* to individual time periods as arise in allocation of costs among years. The issue will not be pressed here, but all conventional revenue recognition methods involve allocation of revenues—usually to a single point in the earnings process, occasionally to more than one point (as when part of the profit is allocated to after costs).[41] As is widely recognized, the earning of revenue is a continuous process from the first point that raw materials are requisitioned to the point when the last related service is performed for the last customer. Allocation of revenues to any *one* point or any *few* points in this process seems subject to the same difficulties as plague allocation of acquisition prices.

But, of course, even without these possible difficulties the arguments presented in this study indicate that in most cases there are at present no theoretically justified ways to make the necessary *expense* determinations. Therefore, at present the "matching" approach is not a promising one.

Despite this, the profession will probably continue to follow the conventional

---

[39] F. K. Wright, "Towards a General Theory of Depreciation," *Journal of Accounting Research*, II (Spring 1964), 82–83.

[40] Another interesting hybrid approach is found in Myron H. Ross, "Depreciation and User Cost," *Accounting Review*, XXXV (July, 1960), 422–28. The method is best explained by using an example similar to the author's. Suppose that a firm buys a machine with a 10-year estimated physical life, and a capacity to produce U units of output. Suppose also that the machine is expected to be obsolete in 5 years. As long as actual outputs are no greater than $U/5$ in any one year, Ross would allocate 1/5th of the acquisition price of the asset to each year (a form of other-services depreciation). But should output increase to a point where the total service life was going to be less than five years, Ross would depreciate the asset in terms of the discounted "foregone future income" sacrificed by obtaining output now instead of later.

[41] See AAA (Matching), p. 371 for an example of this.

matching approach—at least until allocation theory is improved to a point where better allocations become possible at the present level of data aggregation. And, despite the criticisms of practitioners made by theorists, a case can be made that practitioners *should* stick to conventional rules for the present. Although this study has shown that present allocations must be arbitrary, it also has demonstrated that few proposed alternative approaches are significantly better. Arbitrary allocation of a "relevant" figure may be preferable to arbitrary allocation of an irrelevant one. But is it preferable *enough* to warrant the confusions and risks inherent in abandoning historical cost accounting?

Various examples could be given of the costs and dislocations that would result from abandonment of the historical cost rule. Considerable retraining of both accountants and their readers would be necessary. The new rules would tend to affect the reported incomes of different companies with unequal force. There is a potential danger of at least some social dislocation. Financial accounting is part of the system under which a measure of public control over private economic power is sought through disclosure and public scrutiny. As such, it is part of the complicated means by which our present form of capitalism is made palatable to the public. This should make one reluctant to undertake large-scale changes in financial accounting practices unless the resulting benefits are clear and significant.

Accordingly, it may be entirely appropriate to defend the retention of historical costs *even if one believes (as I do) that their use is objectionable from the standpoint of theory*. The need for any large-scale change must exceed a moderately high threshold before change is worthwhile. Otherwise, the losses from abandoning the old methods will exceed the benefits resulting from embracing the new. In light of the conclusions that this study has reached, do the departures from historical cost suggested in the previously cited AAA committee reports (Land, Inventory, Realization, and Matching) attain this threshold? It is an uncomfortable thing to admit, but I doubt that they do.[42]

The exceptions to this (the alternatives *not* affected by the conclusions of this study) all involve substantial changes in the *content* of what is reported. Toward the end of this section it is pointed out that one such change in content is presently in the process of gaining acceptance from the accountant's readers. Otherwise, though, practitioners cannot be expected to move far beyond what their readers would accept without a lengthy period of reader education first.

Diversity in accounting practice

But this does not entitle the profession to ignore that its present allocations *are* arbitrary, and that such arbitrariness cannot be corrected within the present accounting framework. Some response is called for. One possible response (discussed in more detail below) would be to enhance the importance given the funds statement, and to play down the income statement. (Presumably the appropriate *kind* of funds statement to emphasize is the statement of sources and uses of net quick assets: current monetary assets less current liabilities. Such statements make fewer allocations than the usual net-working-capital funds statements.) If this response is not acceptable, then at least the profession should recognize that some of the main argu-

---

[42] I am only too aware that this represents a contradiction of positions that I have taken in the past.

ments supporting the variety of options presently open in reporting nonmonetary economic goods are without substance. Diversity in generally accepted allocation methods is usually defended on four main grounds:[43]

1. Management should be free to use its judgment, since different accounting methods are needed to reflect different economic situations of different firms.

2. Requirement of uniformity would discourage innovation and experimentation.

3. In most cases, as long as one allocation method is followed *consistently*, it makes little difference which allocation method is chosen—therefore any bad effects of diversity are minimal in practice.

4. A requirement of uniformity would create a variety of serious enforcement problems.

The first claim was clearly expressed by Kemp several years ago. His words have been influential and are worth quoting:

> Many depreciation methods are available, but these are not *alternative* methods, as the proponents of "uniformity" seem to believe. . . . The correct method is that one which most nearly accurately describes the using up of the service potential embodied in each asset. Both of the indicated methods may be incorrect, but both certainly cannot be correct. If one is the correct method, then the other is by definition incorrect. The idea that the two methods represent equally acceptable alternatives is ridiculous.
>
> * * *
>
> . . . financial statements should reflect, as nearly accurately as possible, the financial facts concerning a business entity . . . these financial data vary from one company to another and even within a given company. Thus the procedures and methods by which the accounting principles are implemented should not be uniform—indeed, they cannot be.
>
> * * *
>
> A variety of procedures and methods is needed to reflect a variety of circumstances. Various depreciation methods, for example, have been developed to fit a variety of sets of conditions.[44]

But if, within the present framework, nonmonetary goods allocations are at best arbitrary, this claim simply collapses. If allocations cannot be justified anyway, one cannot defend diversity in generally accepted accounting practices as being needed to fit a variety of different circumstances. For *none* of the conflicting approaches will fit. Similarly for the second argument: if allocations cannot be theoretically justified anyway, what is the *point* of innovation and experiment of this kind? Certainly, as has been emphasized before, research is needed. But not research by practitioners into creating new arbitrary methods or new applications of old arbitrary methods.

The third argument is not a positive one *favoring* diversity. It merely is a claim

---

[43] As is often the case, Grady does an excellent job of summarizing conventional informed opinion on this point. See Paul Grady, *Inventory of Generally Accepted Accounting Principles for Business Enterprises*, Accounting Research Study No. 7 (New York: American Institute of Certified Public Accountants, 1965), pp. 32–35. The following comments are mainly intended to raise issues. The uniformity-versus-diversity controversy in accounting is complex—perhaps more complex than the following would suggest. While I favor uniformity, no detailed discussion of the issues is presented since (as indicated below) a radical solution seems even more appropriate: *abandonment* of allocations.

An excellent bibliographical introduction to the uniformity-versus-diversity controversy is Alfred Rappaport, "Seminar Research on Uniformity," *Accounting Review*, XL (July, 1965), 643–48. See also the subsequent "Uniformity in Financial Accounting" issue of *Law and Contemporary Problems*, XXX (Autumn, 1965).

[44] Patrick S. Kemp, "Controversies on the Construction of Financial Statements," *Accounting Review*, XXXVIII (January, 1963), 128, 129, 132.

that if diversity can be defended on *other* grounds, its bad side effects may turn out to be minor. The question then becomes the empirical one of how bad these side effects *are*. At present the evidence is inconclusive.[45] Besides empirical studies, there is an interesting simulation study suggesting that consistency does reduce bad side effects,[46] but there are risks to generalizing from simulation studies—another simulation study (directed to effects of different depreciation approaches for both financial and tax accounting) reaches a different conclusion.[47]

However, some indication of the seriousness of these side effects is provided by the increasing and widely recognized tendency of financial analysts to eliminate at least the *depreciation* allocations from the calculation of net income, and to report "cash flow" income instead. Doubtless, some of this results from efforts by securities salesmen to make firms with poor earnings records appear more attractive to investors, or to compensate for a general market situation in which price-earnings ratios violate traditional rules of thumb; some of this tendency to eliminate depreciation allocations results from misunderstanding of depreciation. But almost certainly much stems from dissatisfaction with the side effects of diversity in accounting. In general, diversity will be *least* apt to have bad side effects when:

1. The purpose of accounting is to report on stewardship—so that comparisons among firms are unimportant.

2. The readers of the financial statements and the firm's management all have interests in the firm that extend over a long period of years—so that short-run advantages of choosing one allocation pattern over another are unlikely to affect decisions.

3. The firm is a "seasoned" one which has reached a stable state in which new assets are acquired regularly, and merely to replace old assets which have been retired. A stable technology must also be assumed. (These requirements, similar to those of Edwards and Bell's stationary state,[48] are sufficient in themselves to eliminate bad side effects of diversity.)

---

[45] First of all, empirical evidence is mixed on whether or not decisions made by readers of financial statements are affected by different allocation approaches. See George C. Holdren, "LIFO and Ratio Analysis," *Accounting Review*, XXXIX (January, 1964), 70–85; Thomas R. Dyckman, "The Effects of Alternative Accounting Techniques on Certain Management Decisions," *Journal of Accounting Research*, II (Spring, 1964), 91–107; and "On the Investment Decision," *Accounting Review*, XXXIX (April, 1964), 285–95; George J. Staubus, "The Association of Financial Accounting Variables With Common Stock Values," *Accounting Review*, XL (January, 1965), 119–34; William J. Bruns, Jr., "Inventory Valuation and Management Decisions," *Accounting Review*, XL (April, 1965), 345–57; Thomas R. Dyckman, "On the Effects of Earnings-Trend, Size and Inventory Valuation Procedures in Evaluating a Business Firm," in Jaedicke, Ijiri, and Nielsen (1966), pp. 175–85; Robert E. Jensen, "An Experimental Design for Study of Effects of Accounting Variations in Decision Making," *Journal of Accounting Research*, IV (Autumn, 1966), 224–38; John Leslie Livingstone, "A Behavioral Study of Tax Allocation in Electric Utility Regulation," *Accounting Review*, XLII (July, 1967), 544–52; George J. Staubus, "Statistical Evidence of the Value of Depreciation Accounting," *Abacus*, III (August, 1967), 3–22; Thomas R. Dyckman, "Observations on Jensen's Experimental Design for Study of Effects of Accounting Variations on Decision Making," *Journal of Accounting Research*, V (Autumn, 1967), 221–29; and Robert E. Jensen, "A Rejoinder," *Journal of Accounting Research*, V (Autumn, 1967), 230–51. For background to several of these studies, see Jacob G. Birnberg and Raghu Nath, "Laboratory Experimentation in Accounting Research," *Accounting Review*, XLIII (January, 1968), 38–45.

[46] Andrew M. McCosh, "Accounting Consistency—Key to Stockholder Information," *Accounting Review*, XLII (October, 1967), 693–700.

[47] Eugene F. Brigham, "The Effects of Alternative Depreciation Policies on Reported Profits," *Accounting Review*, XLIII (January, 1968), 46–61. The reader should note, however, that Brigham offers a possible way to make firms that use different methods comparable with each other (pp. 59–61).

[48] Edwards and Bell (1961), pp. 6–9.

Unfortunately, none of these conditions are as common as their opposites.[49]

In any event, our present toleration of diversity leaves the door open for even greater diversity (and for even greater possible confusion). Elsewhere, I have argued that various novel allocation methods, consistent with present accepted practices, are available to accountants whenever they wish or find it expedient to use them: declining-charge production-basis depreciation, LIFO writeoff of fixed assets; sum-of-the-lunar-months'-digits depreciation of inventories, and so forth. These methods *sound* strange, but really are no more peculiar than certain methods with which we all are familiar.[50]

The fourth argument against uniformity becomes a practical one of enforcement. Enforcement problems would indeed be serious. They would be aggravated by the complexity of business activity and the variety of different situations in which firms become engaged. But if accountants wish to remain within the framework of present conventional accounting, these arguments do not affect the *theoretical* issue of uniformity versus diversity.

Because the present diversity of generally accepted allocation approaches can be defended only on enforcement grounds, this diversity is a disequilibrium situation. Either allocation theory will evolve to a point that the necessary allocations can be theoretically justified or, this diversity will be narrowed. If the profession is unable to enforce the needed restrictions, eventually it will be done by others—the SEC or the courts. *Arbitrary* variety cannot persist forever; eventually, standardization is inevitable.[51]

Possible failure of income determination

But what is standarized will be arbitrary. This study leads to a bleak conclusion

---

[49] Of course, there is another situation in which the side effects of diversity in accounting may not be serious. A company's annual report may sometimes be primarily a public relations tool, and the financial statements themselves may be largely ignored by their recipients. Certain lavish annual reports already seem to be heading in this direction. But this is merely to say that there are circumstances under which accounting theory collapses —something which is true of *any* kind of theory.

[50] The reader who is interested in pursuing these questions should see "The Amortization Problem: A Simplified Model and Some Unanswered Questions," *Journal of Accounting Research*, III (Spring, 1965), 103–13.

[51] A kind of minimum estimate of the *amount* of arbitrary diversity involved here can be made by consulting Grady's chapter on alternative methods—see Grady (1965) Chapter 10. The following list is confined to relatively major alternatives involving allocation.

> Pension payments: two main ways to treat current payments and two main ways to treat past service credits at time of adoption of plan (p. 374).
> Deferred taxes: three ways; also two ways to treat the investment credit (p. 375).
> Depreciation: six ways, applied at at least two different levels of aggregation (p. 375).
> Inventories: at least five ways (p. 376).
> Research, development, and intangible costs: at least two ways (pp. 376–377).
> Leased properties: two ways (p. 378).
> Repair and renewal costs: two ways (p. 379).

The accountant's choices here are independent of each other. For example, his inventory choice does not determine his depreciation choice. So there are a minimum of:

$$(2 \times 2) \times (2 \times 3) \times (6 \times 2) \times (5) \times (2) \times (2) \times (2)$$

or 11,520 major alternative sets of "generally accepted" accounting practices involving allocation. Grady's list is conservative; one could easily obtain a much higher total. Sterling, only partly tongue-in-cheek, calculates that there are 9,720 different costs for LIFO alone. . . see Robert R. Sterling, "In Defense of Accounting in the United States," *Abacus*, II (December, 1966), 181. I suspect that the number of alternative sets of allocation practices far exceeds the number of corporations doing business in the United States.

that may be stated briefly. Three generations of accountants have tried to provide theoretical justification to different ways of giving operational meaning to the economists' abstract concepts of "profits" and income. To date, these efforts have failed—except perhaps for one approach that ill agrees with one's implicit notions of income, and which does not always seem germane to reader decisions. It should be emphasized again that this conclusion pertains only to the present conditions of accounting theory and allocation theory. At any time an intellectual breakthrough could reverse this conclusion. I have previously mentioned promising research that is being done in relating accounting to developments in measurement science, communication theory, and the behavioral sciences. *But it is high time that we also consider the possibility of ultimate failure in our efforts to determine income.* Income determination may not really be as necessary as most accountants believe. An alternative is available—one that already has been closely explored from both the theoretical and the practical standpoint. Besides avoiding the allocation problem, there is a good chance that this alternative would be acceptable to most readers of financial statements.

Financial accounting would be no worse off than it is now, and probably would be *better* off, were the income concept abandoned. Funds statements (preferably net-quick-assets funds statements, of the kind described in Appendix B to this chapter) still could be prepared; as is well known, in a crude way this is just what is being done *now* by analysts dissatisfied with financial accounting's allocations.[52] The arguments developed in this study demonstrate that insofar as present income reporting goes *beyond* the data presented on a net-quick-assets funds statement, the additional figures reported are almost always arbitrary. Future research *may* improve the quality of these figures. But at present little would be lost by preparing funds statements instead of income statements. And if, as seems likely, readers are being confused by financial accounting's allocations, much might be gained by the change.[53]

This study has demonstrated that these allocations are arbitrary—and that they will continue to be arbitrary for the foreseeable future. Therefore the reader is invited to perform another mental experiment. Suppose that a large publicly held corporation were each year to determine an Optional Factor (the name is meaningless) to be prominently and separately displayed at the bottom of the annual income statement. The O-factor would be determined by consulting a table of random numbers, under the constraint that it be somewhere between 2 percent and 20 percent of the company's average reported net income over the past five years. What would readers of financial statements do with this O-factor?

Doubtless many would just ignore it. Others, though, would worry about it and waste time. Almost certainly other readers would compare the current year's O-factor with those of prior years and try to use the results in their decision processes.

---

[52] See, for example, Allan R. Drebin, " 'Cash-Flowitis': Malady or Syndrome?" *Journal of Accounting Research,* II (Spring, 1964), 25–34. Drebin's article is one of relatively few in the accounting literature that is more concerned with the implications of this phenomenon than with denouncing it. One's reaction to cash-flow accounting *should* be similar to one's reaction to "bootleg" bookkeeping (which it resembles): as a symptom of possible inadequacies in the "official" system, not as something reprehensible.

[53] See Staubus (1965), pp. 120, 121, 127, 129, 133, 134. See also Howard C. Greer, "The Corporation Stockholder—Accounting's Forgotten Man," *Accounting Review,* XXXIX (January, 1964), 22–31, for less empirical arguments to the same point. Greer attempts a rough estimate of the extent of confusion possible under current allocation rules (see pp. 27–28 especially).

On the average, annual disclosure of this O-factor would leave readers a little worse off than they are under present disclosure rules.

Considering the discussion of "blurring" in Chapter Four, and of among-years interaction effects in Chapter Five, the disservice done by financial accounting's allocations probably exceeds that done by this imaginary O-factor, though our familiarity with the allocations usually blinds us to this. And the arbitrary elements in our allocations are intimately mingled with the rest of the report, not kept separate. No responsible accountant would recommend inclusion of an O-factor in the annual report. Perhaps we accountants should stop allocating, too.

An appeal to laymen

What follows is tentative. Most data given to laymen are presented in ways that circumvent the necessity to deal with interaction. We hear of the number of touchdowns that a quarterback has made. Strictly speaking, this is nonsense—most football plays are complicated networks of interactions in which the contribution of any one player rarely is sufficient to explain the result. But sports reporting concentrates on the ball carrier—probably because at the time of the play he is the most interesting figure to the *spectators*. Similarly, battles are described in terms of the decisions of generals; female beauty (mostly a matter of the *relationships* of anatomical features, not their absolute magnitudes) is often represented by three measurements; and so forth. Many other examples could be offered. In each case, interaction considerations are avoided by couching the discussion in terms of a single aspect (or at most a very few aspects) deemed to be of particular interest to readers.

In Chapter One it was pointed out that financial accounting could be theoretically justified by appealing to rules upon which intelligent laymen would agree—that accounting rules would be justified if they were consequences of propositions which lay readers of accounting reports would concede. It follows that a system of reporting economic data would be theoretically justified if it avoided interaction considerations in a manner that paralleled the treatment given them in other accepted kinds of reporting to laymen. Cash-flow accounting seems to do exactly this: it avoids interaction considerations by concentrating on a single aspect of economic activity that is of particular interest to lay readers (and, for that matter, of particular int rest to management during the actual economic activity itself). Thus the substitution of net-quick-assets funds statements for income statements might be defended on positive grounds, as well as on the largely negative ones given above. Unfortunately, this argument is not decisive. This is partly for reasons that are given in the next section, partly because most intelligent laymen would be distressed by some features of cash-flow accounting. For example, most laymen presumably believe it appropriate to recognize a gain or loss on the incidental sale of a fixed asset; yet such recognition is barred under cash-flow accounting.

Another appeal to laymen

There is one final way in which appeal might be made to "rules upon which intelligent laymen would agree." Suppose that laymen were asked, say, the appropriate way to allocate the cost of a depreciable asset to its years of service life. Suppose also that the alternatives were carefully explained and the possibility of not allocating at all was explicitly permitted. I hypothesize that a large proportion of intelligent lay-men would recommend abandoning depreciation entirely—to many people, depre-ciation seems "something that the accountant worries about," and has little personal significance. I hypothesize that most of the remaining laymen would recommend some form of straight-line depreciation. What is important is that one's hypotheses can be *tested* here, and some definite result obtained.[54]

Suppose that laymen agree that straight-line depreciation was the appropriate way to allocate the depreciable asset's cost. Then, straight-line depreciation satisfies two of the minimum criteria for theoretical justification of an allocation method (de-veloped in Chapter One). It *does* allocate the asset's cost. It *is* defensible (one might suspect that the laymen were responding to some form of Bernoulli's principle, or to some implicit assumption of equal benefits in each year; but any such suspicions would be irrelevant to the question of whether a successful appeal to laymen had been made).

Unfortunately, there would still be problems of ambiguity. As Chapter One also pointed out, for a depreciation method to be theoretically justified it must be unam-bigous; yet there are *several* straight-line methods. Besides the one ordinarily so designated, both the production method and the group method may be regarded as straight-line approaches. A case can be made that at least one increasing-charge method is a straight-line approach, too (this is the particular increasing charge method that is designed to give a constant return on beginning-of-year book value). Assuming again that the alternatives were adequately explained, I suspect that laymen might find *all* of these alternatives acceptable—because laymen would respond in terms of broad aesthetic and ethical desires for symmetry and fairness, rather than any-thing that would lead to selection of one of the straight-line approaches to the exclu-sion of all others. But until these beliefs have been tested, the point should not be pressed beyond observing that an appeal to laymen will fail unless the criterion unambiguity is satisfied—and that there is a *general* danger that lay opinions about accounting are neither sufficiently consistent nor sufficiently clear-cut to avoid am-biguity.[55]

What if, as is likely, laymen *dis*agreed? Suppose that, say, after the alternatives were carefully explained, 51 percent of the laymen sampled favored straight-line depreciation, 39 percent favored no depreciation at all, and 10 percent were unde-cided (suppose also that enough sampling had been done to reduce the sampling error to insignificance). Should we then make *another* appeal to laymen, and adopt ma-jority rule? The criteria of theoretical justification might be met, but would we be content with the result?

This leads to a final observation. If accountants *were* to appeal to laymen for their allocation rules, thereafter accountants would have to admit that a major part of their financial statements no longer provided economic information, except to the extent that the beliefs of intelligent laymen may be consistent with economics. But

---

[54] The development and pilot test of such a study might provide a doctoral dissertation topic for someone. Presumably it would be necessary to give "intelligent laymen" the usual operational meaning of "college stu-dents, leaders of the business community, and individuals willing to fill out questionnaires."

[55] Any attempt to appeal to rules which lay *readers of financial statements* accept presumably would lead to at least as much ambiguity. Such an appeal would also be subject to the difficulty mentioned in the next paragraph.

then why should someone seeking economic information about the firm consult accounting's allocations?[56]

All considered, an effort might be made to base financial accounting allocations on rules which intelligent laymen would find acceptable. The suggestion offers enough promise to justify the effort necessary to test the related hypotheses. But I anticipate that neither accountants nor lay users of financial statements would be satisfied with the results.

Summary

. . . my own guess is that, so far as the history of accounting is concerned, the next twenty-five years may subsequently be seen to have been the twilight of income measurement.[57]

In the present state of accounting theory and allocation theory, there usually will be only a few ways to escape the problems discussed in this book. Accountants might stop reporting economic information about nonmonetary goods (in the sense discussed immediately above). Or accountants might stop allocating.

The possible ways to stop allocating have been discussed: the current-price valuation approaches recommended by Chambers and Sterling, and the substitution of net-quick-assets funds statements for income statements. Of course these two approaches are not mutually exclusive. The funds statement approach could employ a current-price balance sheet (though doing so would destroy the present agreement between changes in magnitudes reported on the balance sheet, and the magnitudes reported on the income statement). Both of these ways to stop allocating lead to other difficulties. Both lead to abandoning the effort to measure income—either to abandoning it explicitly, or to doing so *de facto* by following rules that violate the usual conceptions of the nature of income measurement.

The final alternative is to ignore the problem. Accountants may be content to perform arbitrary allocations—that is, to continue doing what they are doing now. The main drawback to arbitrary allocations is that the significance of reported magnitudes becomes impossible to specify. Accordingly, accountants seem to be faced with three main alternatives. They must either:

1. Stop reporting economic information about nonmonetary goods and their amor-

---

[56] To be sure, economics developed historically out of "the beliefs of intelligent laymen." But, like most other kinds of specialized knowledge, it has left its lay origins far behind. Medicine is a parallel case; at *some* period, medicine developed out of the beliefs of intelligent laymen, too. But in both cases an appeal to lay opinion would often prove unsatisfactory now.

The comments in this section have been directed toward "laymen" in general, but they also apply to appeals made to specific *kinds* of laymen, such as public utility commissioners, judges, and framers of tax regulations. For example, Brigham concludes that most public utility commissioners favor straight-line depreciation—see Brigham (1968), p. 50n. Presumably, the *type* of straight-line depreciation is unambiguous in this case. But will reports based on the commissioners' depreciation preferences be significant to a reader who is seeking economic information? The generally poor reputation of accounting for regulated industries suggests otherwise. Similar remarks could be made about the kinds of accounting embodied in judicial opinions and tax laws.

Finally, it could be argued that in regulated industries, the commissioners both have assumed many of the responsibilities of management *and* tend to reflect many of the attitudes and goals of management. In such cases, an appeal to the commissioners' depreciation preferences has many of the earlier noted defects of an appeal to management's depreciation preferences. Similarly, the law tends to embody whatever common industry practice may be at some point in time.

[57] David Solomons, "Economic and Accounting Concepts of Income," *Accounting Review*, XXXVI (July, 1961), 383.

tization (except insofar as the beliefs of intelligent laymen are consistent with economics); or,

2. Abandon the effort to measure income; or,

3. Allow a large part (probably the *major* part) of their financial statements to be nearly void of meaningful content.

The first of these alternatives will be theoretically justified only if the opinions of intelligent laymen about accounting are consistent and unambiguous—which seems unlikely. The second alternative suffers from all the weaknesses that characterize the related substitute measures. Unfortunately, the third alternative is always possible.

Financial accounting theory began to take its present form around the turn of the century. It crystalized into what are now the various orthodox rules and ways of perceiving things by the 1930's. Recently, signs of major change have become visible. Perhaps the majority of academic theorists now reject the historical cost rule. And many theorists are attempting far more sweeping changes than this. Many writers, especially the younger theorists, are trying to reconstruct financial accounting on entirely new foundations.

This book has ended with some very gloomy conclusions. But they pertain only to the ways in which we *now* perceive accounting. A long winter of orthodoxy seems to be nearing its end. It is impossible to say what the new accounting will be like. But most of the problems discussed in this book are unlikely to survive the thaw.

APPENDIX A

The Validity of This Study

This study is an extended piece of deductive reasoning. Long deductive arguments are terribly fragile: it takes just one error in their premises or reasoning to invalidate them. No such argument can be considered proved until it has been exposed to criticism for several years. I am twice on record as recommending that there be more give and take in accounting theory:

Compared with other learned disciplines, accounting controversy is usually conducted in a remarkably gentlemanly manner. It is as though the reasons which ordinarily prevent accounting firms from being unpleasant to each other applied with equal force to accounting professors. It could be argued that a bit more venom in accounting writing would tend to discourage carelessness . . .[58]

Turnabout is fair play. If there are any mistakes in this study, it is hoped that they will be pointed out, publicly and with vigor. To help such criticism along, this study will conclude by raising as many questions as possible about its own validity. This is not done out of any personal unease about my reasoning. Instead, the point is that most previous accounting theory has fallen prey to errors, or to assumptions that are subject to challenge. Although I'm convinced that my own reasoning is correct and well grounded, it is desirable for once to make the possibilities of error explicit. What follows is expressed as a series of questions. I hope that the following is a reasonably

---

[58] " 'Value-itis'—An Impractical Theorist's Reply." *Accounting Review*, XXXIX (July, 1964), 574; see also letter, *Journal of Accountancy*, CXX (July, 1965), 17.

complete list of possible trouble spots in the argument . . . but of course this is something only the reader himself can decide.

1. At the level of aggregation found in present financial statements, are interaction effects as widespread and important as asserted? Is there evidence to the contrary that has not been discussed? Are there a significant number and variety of firms with revenue functions that incorporate few or no interactions? How sensitive are actual allocations to the presence of minor interactions? Is the dismissal of the allocation problems of monetary goods warranted? or do these goods significantly interact with each other or with nonmonetary goods?

2. At what level of aggregation do actual revenue functions typically become free of significant interaction effects? Is it necessary to compress financial statement data as much as has been suggested in this study, or would less drastic compression permit theoretically justified allocation? In particular, many published income statements *presently* are quite compressed; often they report only three or four main expense categories (cost of goods sold, selling expenses, administrative expenses, taxes). Might this compression suffice?

3. In answering the previous questions, it should be kept in mind that interaction is an among-years as well as a within-year problem; how serious is the interaction problem among years for actual revenue functions? What are the actual effects of dynamic relationships and other among-year phenomena mentioned on the revenue function?

4. In statistics, it is often possible to determine some of the separate effects of different factors, even when these factors are correlated. Similarly, to what extent is it possible to distinguish separate inputs once they have joined the common pool of nonmonetary economic goods? In the language of this study, how badly *do* goods (and related expenses) really "blur" into each other? As a practical question, assuming that separate effects can be partly distinguished, what are the data requirements for reducing blurring to tolerable dimensions?

5. In Chapter One, there is a basic description of current financial accounting practice. In Chapter Two, there is a basic description of present depreciation theory and practice. In Chapter Six, there is a description of the main approaches to income determination that have been employed or suggested in accounting. Are these descriptions correct? do they fit the reader's own experience of financial accounting and its literature?

6. Is there some interpretation by which the accountant's treatment of nonmonetary economic goods does not involve allocation—an interpretation by which theoretical justification might be given to that treatment? (In particular, can a different interpretation be given to inventory amortization and write-offs of other nondurable nonmonetary goods—an interpretation that would escape the difficulties discussed in this study?) Are there interaction-free models of the relationship between entity inputs and income which have not been discussed in this study, and which could be adapted to the financial accountant's needs? Three main approaches to allocation are discussed in Chapter Three. Is there some theoretical approach to allocation not discussed in this study that might avoid the difficulties that have been examined? (For instance, were research to develop a clearer picture of the behavioral effects of financial statements on investors, would this provide an alternative approach to reporting that would avoid allocation problems?)

7. Is there some other form of the net-revenue-contributions approach that this study has overlooked, and which would escape the difficulties associated with the forms that *are* discussed? Does the appeal to laymen and economists for theoretical justification leave out any other significant group to which appeal might be made? Has some way been overlooked to defend the assumption of constant returns to scale at the level of aggregation faced by the accountant? Is the argument correct that constant returns to scale are necessary for the marginal contributions approach? Is there some way to incorporate fixed factors in a Cobb-Douglas function in a manner consistent with the financial accountant's needs? Are there any current-price valuation approaches other than ones similar to those proposed by Chambers and Sterling that avoid allocations, or that allocate, but can justify their allocations in a conclusive fashion? Is the description of the difficulties involved in an appeal to laymen correct? Has any of the recent research in communication theory, behavioral science, or measurement science reached a point where it can be regarded as offering a serious alternative to conventional accounting theory, and one which solves the allocation problem? Is any such solution forthcoming in the near future? Have any major arguments favoring diversity in accounting practice been overlooked in the discussion?

8. It is possible to interpret rates of return either as costs of capital or as target rates that approximate an opportunity rate. No attempt has been made in this study to distinguish different effects of these two interpretations; do the conclusions reached hold under either interpretation? Similarly, does the choice of an "income" instead of a "cash-flow" interpretation of an input's services affect any of the conclusions reached? In general, any author inevitably gives certain interpretations to concepts and ignores others. Do any of the conclusions in this study hinge on the particular interpretation given to some key concept?

Is the ignoring of multiple yields appropriate? Does the ignoring of estimation difficulties somehow lead the arguments in this study to incorrect conclusions? The distinctions made among production, market, revenue, cost, and income functions are important in the argument; are these concepts applied consistently and appropriately?

9. The arguments developed in this study have tried to demonstrate that financial accounting's matching and cost-accumulation activities lack theoretical justification. To what extent is theoretical justification really necessary? Is it really important that accountants be able to defend all steps in their matching and cost-accumulation practices? or *can* one say, and does it *suffice* to say, that some arbitrary approaches are superior to others? Accounting is often perceived as a model of economic activity; all models distort. How arbitrary can accounting be without losing effectiveness as a model? do we presently have any way to answer this question? Are the "minimum requirements" to theoretically justify an allocation method all really necessary? Much of this study depends on the implications drawn from these requirements. Are there any logical errors, unintentional shifts of meaning, hidden assumptions, or other fallacies here? *Is* there any way to justify allocations that ignore part of what is there to be allocated? Are the discussions of satisficing, surrogates, and decisions under ignorance correct? Is the claim correct that at present there is no unanimity concerning purposes to be served by accounting (except at a level that is too vague to be of help in allocation decisions), or concerning priorities of purposes?

Appendix B

Net-Quick-Asset Funds Statements

To avoid possible confusion, the following is a brief discussion of the kind of "cash-flow income" reporting recommended in this chapter. A net-quick-assets funds statement is constructed in the same way as the familiar statement of sources and uses of net working capital, except that nonmonetary current assets (inventories and prepayments) are not treated as "fund" assets. In the simplified example below data have been rounded and a few zeros discarded.

Exhibit 6-1

Miami Corporation
Summary of Major Economic Events
For 19×1

1. Sales totalled $2,160; cost of goods sold was calculated as $1,200; the company purchased inventories costing $1,180.
2. Interest charges totalled $80; miscellaneous current costs of operations totalled $480.
3. Depreciation was $240 on equipment and $30 on buildings.
4. Used equipment having a book value of $300 was sold for $220; land that had cost $60 was sold for $290.
5. The company declared and paid $200 of dividends.
6. The company purchased $670 of equipment and $100 of buildings.
7. The company issued additional capital stock for $500 and bonds payable for $100, cash. The company made a $300 payment on the principal of its mortgage payable.

Exhibit 6-2

Miami Corporation
Income Statement
For 19×1

Revenues:		
Sales..		$2,160
Expenses:		
Cost of Goods Sold.................................	$1,200	
Depreciation Expense...............................	270	
Interest Expense...................................	80	
Miscellaneous Expense..............................	480	2,030
Net income from operations........................		$ 130
Non-operating gains and losses:		
Gain on Sale of Land...............................	$ 230	
Loss on Sale of Equipment..........................	80	150
Net income..		$ 280
Dividends..		200
Increase in Retained Earnings......................		$ 80

Exhibit 6-3

MIAMI CORPORATION
SOURCES AND USES OF NET QUICK ASSETS
FOR 19×1

SOURCES

Funds from operations:
  Receipts:
    Sales..$2,160
  Expenditures:

Purchases of inventories............	$1,180	
Interest charges....................	80	
Miscellaneous costs of operations....	480	1,740

  Funds from operations.............................. $ 420

Proceeds from sale of noncurrent assets:

Sale of equipment...................	$ 220	
Sale of land........................	290	510

Proceeds from issue of noncurrent equities

Capital stock.......................	$ 500	
Bonds payable.......................	100	600

  Net sources..................................... $1,530

USES

Purchase of noncurrent assets:

Equipment...........................	$ 670	
Buildings...........................	100	$ 770

Retirement of noncurrent equities:
  Payment made on mortgage principal................. 300
Dividends declared.................................... 200

  Net uses.. $1,270

  Increase in net quick assets during year. $ 260

Exhibit 6-3 has been expressed in a fairly conventional funds-statement form (but without the usual supplementary schedule of changes in fund accounts). It should be noted that the purchases of inventory have been included in the calculation of funds from operations, rather than among the purchases of equipment and buildings.

If this kind of funds statement were substituted for the income statement, it might be desirable to preserve some of the income statement language to which stockholders are presently accustomed. Exhibit 6-4 shows one of the several ways in which this might be done.

Exhibit 6-4

Miami Corporation
Current Operating Profit
And Other Major Economic Activities
For 19×1

Sales..		$2,160
Expenditures:		
Cost of goods...	$1,180	
Interest..	80	
Miscellaneous..	480	1,740
CURRENT OPERATING PROFIT..................		$ 420
Replacement and expansion of plant (net of proceeds from sale		
of retired plant assets)...............................	$ 260	
Dividends declared....................................	200	460
Net decrease in funds before financing...................		$ (40)
Long-term financing of company operations:		
Capital stock issued..................................	$ 500	
Bonds payable issued................................	100	
Total new long-term financing........................	$ 600	
Less: Payment made on mortgage principal...............	300	300
Increase in net quick assets during 19×1...............		$ 260

Footnotes that would ordinarily accompany Exhibit 6–4 have been omitted. I have no particular stake in the form or language employed in Exhibit 6–4; both might be improved. The important feature of this illustration is its prominent calculation of the $420 Current Operating Profit figure, whatever label is given to it.

Index